Finding Bombay:

Experiencing the Soul of Bombay Through Its Food

By:

Chef and Restauranteur,

Zubin E. Kolah

Finding Bombay:
Experiencing the Soul of Bombay
Through Its Food

Copyright © 2017 by Zubin E. Kolah. All rights reserved.

Designed and Printed by Clearstory Digital Printing
in the United States of America.

No part of this publication may be reproduced,
stored in a retrieval system or transmitted in any form
or by any means, electronic, mechanical, photocopying,
recording, or otherwise, without the prior written
permission of the publisher. For permission, contact
the legal department at Malabar Hill Publishing, LLC
in writing to 3952 D Clairemont Mesa Boulevard, Ste. 161,
San Diego, California 92117, U.S.A.

Photographs by
Lee Sie Photography and Quinn LaCasse Photography.
Published by: Malabar Hill Publishing, LLC
ISBN-978-0-9991285-0-3

TABLE OF CONTENTS

HISTORY — 13

Geography 4	*The Food* 15	*My Culinary Kaleidoscope* 10
The People 5	*A Culture within a Culture* 9	

THE BASICS — 13

Cooking Times 15	*Curry* 17	*Garam Masala* 22
Equipment 15	*Tamarind* 18	*Garlic-Ginger Paste* 25
Tandoori Cooking 15	*Saffron* 18	*Tandoori Masala* 26
Choosing Ingredients 16	*Spices* 21	

APPETIZERS — 29

Aloo Pattice 32	Paneer Pakoda 40	Samosas 47
Chicken Lollipops 35	Pappadums 43	Veggie Balls 48
Eggplant Cutlets 36	Raisin Aloo Paneer Rolls 44	
Onion Bhajias 39		

MEAT RECIPES (LAMB) MEMANA — 51

Lamb Chop 54	Lamb Kathi Roll 58	Lamb Shank 62
Lamb Curry 57	Lamb Seekh Kebab 61	Kashmiri Lamb Rogan Josh 65

MEAT RECIPES (CHICKEN) MURGH — 66

Achari Murgh 66	Chicken Korma 72	Chicken Tikka Masala 79
Balti Chicken Pasanda 69	Dry Jeera Chicken 75	Chicken Vindaloo 80
Chicken Curry 70	Chicken Tikka Kebab 76	East Indian Chicken Curry 82

MEAT RECIPES CONTINUED

Garlic Chicken Dry 85	Mango Chicken Masala 90	Reshmi Kebab 97
Honey Lemon Chicken 86	Methi Murgh 93	Saffron Chicken 98
Karahi Chicken 89	Murgh Musallam 94	Tandoori Chicken 101

FISH & SHRIMP MACHHALEE & JHEENGA   103

A Visit to the Fish Market in Bombay 105	Fish Cakes 113	Madras Fish Curry 121
Cheese Fish Fillets with Hot Tomato Sauce 108	Fish in Coconut Milk 114	Malabar Shrimp Curry 122
Dum Jhinga Anari 110	Grilled King Prawn 117	Shrimp Kebab 125
	Jhinga Malai Curry 118	Tandoori Fish 127

VEGETARIAN SHAAKAAHAAREE   129

Paneer 132	Dal & Spinach 143	Paneer Makhani 153
Aloo Gobi 135	Kadhai Paneer 145	Paneer Tawa Masala 154
Aloo Jeera 136	Kofta Curry 146	Punjabi Dal 157
Baingan Bharta 139	Navrattan Korma 149	
Channa Masala 140	Palak Paneer 150	

RICE DISHES CHAAVAL   159

Boiled Basmati Rice 163	Green Peas & Mushroom Rice 167	Lamb Pulao 170
Chicken Biryani 164	Herb, Shrimp & Rice Pulao 168	South Indian Lemon Rice 173

INDIAN BREADS ROTEE 175

Bhatura/Pooris 179	Plain Paratha 183	Whole Wheat Chappatis 187
Naan 180	Stuffed Parathas 184	

PARSI DISHES 189

Chicken Liver Gravy with Gizzards 192	Kheema Curry 204	Marghi-na-Farcha 214
Dhansak Dal 194	Kera-per-eda 207	Mutton Kebab 216
Egg Curry 196	Fried Brown Rice 208	Parsi Poro 219
Fish Tamatar 200	Kolmi-no-patio 210	Patra-ni-Machi 220
Green Chicken Curry 203	Lamb Jardalo Salli Boti 212	Tareli Machi 223

CHUTNEYS & RELISHES CHATANEE AUR SVAAD 225

Mint Chutney 229	Tamarind Chutney 233	Kachumbar 237
Spicy Red Chutney 230	Cabbage Salad 234	Peach Chutney 238
		Yogurt Raita 241

INDIAN DESSERTS & DRINKS 243

Falooda 246	Khoya 254	Parsi Sev 262
Gajar Halwa 249	Lagan-nu-Custard 257	Masala Chai 265
Gulab Jamun 250	Mango Ice Cream 258	Sweet Lassi 266
Kheer 253	Mango Mousse 261	Mango Lassi 266

CONVERSION GUIDE 268   INDEX 270

Traditional Indian and Parsi recipes from my childhood and modernist Indian dishes I make at my restaurants in California…

…none of which would be possible without the blessing of being born to my parents, Eruch and Coomi, who put me on a path of unlimited love and absolute support even from the other side of the world. This book is dedicated to them.

Thanks Mom and Dad.

HISTORY

Fish market

To know the cuisine of a culture one has to know the people, and to know the people one has to know their history. The history of Bombay and its people bore out of more than just India.

Bombay is everyone who has landed on her shores to partake in her rich giving of land, fortunes, spices, natural resources and human labor. Bombay's origins combine several governing nations with their vibrant cultural footprint left behind to influence the indigenous and migrant people of today's Bombay.

The fisher folk, known as the Kolis, are a Marathi fishing community and were the earliest settlers of the islands of Bombay. Thereafter, until 1534, Bombay belonged to the Hindu rulers of India.

However, in 1534, the Treaty of Bassein granted the island of Bassein and the seven islands that made up Bombay to the Portuguese in order to stay the power of the Mughal emperor Humayun.

Later, the 1661 Treaty of Whitehall gifted Bombay to Charles II of England as a dowry for Catherine of Braganza's (daughter to the King of Portugal) marriage to Charles II.

Seven years later, in 1668, Charles II happily gave Bombay over to the fledgling merchant business The East India Company in order to thwart the rising Dutch Empire and transfer the expensive maintenance that Charles II incurred from "inheriting" Bombay.

The East India Company not only inherited a rich port, they inherited one of many pots of gold that would allow them to become the first mega-corporation in the modern history of the world, which would grow to run trade in all the emerging nations.

Geography

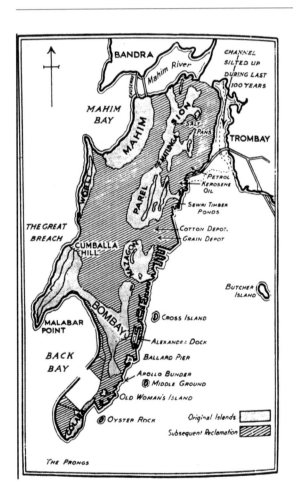

Bombaia—Good Bay, as Portuguese explorer Francisco de Almeida named it, sits on the central western coast of India and the Arabian Ocean and consists of an archipelago of seven islands: Bombay Island, Parel, Mazagoan, Mahim, Worli, Colaba, and Old Woman's Island.

In the bay, due to the torrential floods of the summer monsoons many of the smaller islands were visible only parts of the year. The Portuguese also called the islands Mombayn, Bombay, Bombain, Bombaym, Monbaym, Mombai, Mombay, Bombeye, Boon Bay, and Bon Bahia.

Bombay's sheltered deep-water harbor made it a prized possession amongst the ruling nations at the time of takeover by the East India Company. It was during British rule that the islands were connected by a mega land reclamation project. During the 17th Century, the British anglicized the Portuguese term of Bombaim to Bombay.

In 1995, Hindu nationalist sentiment caused the re-naming of Indian cities. Specifically, in the state of Maharashtra, where Bombay is located, the Koli's mother tongue and the state's official language of Marathi dictated that Bombay be changed to Mumbai. Mumbai is derived from Mumbadevi—the name of the patron goddess and protector of the Koli.

Street side vendor making Pav Bhaji in Bombay

The People

Bombay has been shaped by the influence of the Dutch, the Portuguese, Muslims, the Hindus, the Parsee, the Sikh, the British, and indigenous sects. It also has a rich Indian-Chinese history. Many restaurants in Bombay have numerous offerings of Indian-Chinese dishes alongside the Indian staples. Today, Bombay, which is roughly forty miles (65 kilometers) in area, contains 22 million people.

The Food

Bombay is probably the only city in India where food from any part of the country and the world can be found. The streets are vibrant with various sounds of old traditions mixed with new. There are Western fast food franchises strewn throughout the city like McDonalds®, Kentucky Fried Chicken®, Pizza Hut®, Subway®, and Baskin Robbins®, to name a few.

But, the dominant features of the culinary landscape are the traditional Indian dishes served in a myriad of ways, plus traditional dishes made with other cultural ingredients and techniques that have formed original and uniquely Bombay cuisine.

Marine Drive, aka, Queen's Necklace, Mumbai

There are street hawkers that have been in business for many generations, starting off with a small cart and then finally being able to acquire a whole corner of the street. Bombay never sleeps. The various types of cuisines can be found anywhere in Bombay. The street food of Bombay is everyday food sold to people rushing to work, coming off the overcrowded trains, all ages of youngsters with their backpacks full of books heavier than they are, and everyone else moving in a systematic chaos of unending life.

The street food of Bombay is fast and fresh because it's made right in front of you in a few minutes and absolutely delicious. The prices are rock bottom, the lines of people are the standard and the variety of food suits every craving. Vada pav, pani puri, bhel puri, sev puri, sandwiches, chai, idlis and dosas, onion pakora, and even sweets and drinks like kulfi (ice cream), falooda, lassi, sweet lime juice and sugarcane juice are available fast and easy on the streets of Bombay.

Along with various street foods, one can find restaurants serving the western coastal cuisine, which is a Konkan cuisine. Konkan cuisine is a mix of coconut, spices, tangy and starchy dishes along with fish curries.

Many restaurants serve North Indian cuisine. North Indian food is also called Punjabi cuisine. This cuisine uses dairy products in many of their dishes, along with saffron, chillies and nuts. The use of the "tawa" (griddle) for baking flat roti and paratha is also used in North Indian cooking. And the "tandoor" clay oven is synonymous with this regional cuisine. Goat and lamb meats are used in many recipes. One of the most popular North Indian finger snacks is the deep fried samosa and it comes with a variety of filings including potato, minced meat, paneer, mushroom or chick pea.

There are a handful of long-time and iconic restaurants in Bombay that serve this cuisine so you remember the taste ten, twenty, even thirty years later and it tastes the same. Growing up in Bombay, my family and I ate out at these restaurants only on special occasions.

However, even though times have changed and eating out is an everyday thing in our busy and connected world, the food and the familial special occasions have not—each time we visit family in Bombay, we eat at the same restaurants. Sharing in the dishes of my childhood reaches back into my mind and pulls the warmest memories and sensory emotions to the front of my heart.

Some of the more popular dishes familiar in the West consist of chicken tikka masala, chicken curry, lamb curry, goat curry, paneer bhurji, saag paneer, navrattan korma, aloo gobi, channa masala, malai kofta and a rice preparation generically called biryani.

Not to forget about the delicious tandoor clay oven bread, the most internationally famous of them being the plain butter naan. Other beautiful dough creations are roomali roti (the thinnest and most buttery flat bread eaten with the hand—as you pull it the elasticity of the dough makes for a light chewiness), garlic naan, parathas and rotis. However, in Bombay the international staples of Punjabi food are accompanied by dozens of offerings of typical Bombay Punjabi dishes known in cosmopolitan areas of India, but, virtually unknown elsewhere. The other dishes are mutton cream tikka, reshmi kebab, mutton sheikh kebab, tandoori prawns, paneer achari tikka, chicken farcha, egg masala, bheja (brain) masala, and prawns fry to name just a few.

North Indian cuisine does not come at a cost of excluding South Indian food in Bombay. South Indian cuisine is distinguished by the staples of rice, sambar, rasam, various pickles, coconut and curry leaves. For example, idli-dosa menus are found throughout the city and can turn anyone into a vegetarian.

The most common misconception about Indian food is that it is so spicy such that one needs to be prepared for a run to the restroom after eating. However, chili pepper was not native to the Indian subcontinent. The Portuguese introduced Mexican chili pepper to India.

Bombay's South Indian cuisine hails from Andhra Pradesh, Kerala, Karnataka and Tamil Nadu. They serve breakfast treats like idli, dosa and uttapas with coconut chutney and sambhar many, many more dishes are part of the category of South Indian cuisine. The amount of vegetarian dishes boggles the mind and one would not miss being a meat-eater if they had to rely on South Indian cuisine for their sustenance.

Baking chicken in tandoor oven

Indian-Chinese food, or Indo-Chinese originated around the late 1700s in Calcutta. Yang Tai Chow was the first recorded Chinese to migrate to India via land route from China to Calcutta. The Chinese soon assimilated many Indian ways and fused their cooking with popular Indian recipes. The spice and oil ingredients made for a perfect marriage as both cuisines utilize them. For example, paneer morphed into Schezwan paneer, chicken curry became chili chicken, aloo bhindi transformed into Kung Pao potatoes with okra in a sweet and spicy tomato based dry sauce.

Other popular dishes include veg Manchurian dry, veg paneer, gobi Manchurian, veg Manchow soup, Schezwan noodles, veg Hakka noodles, chili baby corn gravy, sweet corn soup, dim sum and veg balls in hot garlic-ginger paste sauce. There is even a mix of Indo-Chinese cooking with Malaysian, Thai, Burmese and Vietnamese cuisines.

Centuries of various European occupations of Bombay has led to a culinary infusion as well. The British introduced tea and baking to India, and the introduction of meat and fish by Christians. Bombay has many high-end restaurants that offer authentic Western dishes. There are also famous everyday Western restaurants like Leopold Café located on the Colaba Causeway. One can find Italian, French, Spanish, Portuguese, Russian, Mediterranean, Mexican, and typical American fare.

It would be an injustice to discuss the other cuisines of Bombay in a simple paragraph. They are worthy of their own cookbooks, each of which I intend to cover in my next cookbooks.

Coomi & Eruch Kolah, 1999, eating off banna leaves at my traditional Parsi wedding

A Culture Within a Culture

Several hundred years ago, Persian Zoroastrians fled Iran to avoid religious persecution by invaders (a conquest more than 1000 years after the establishment of the Zoroastrians). The Zoroastrians fled via the Arabian Sea towards India. They landed on the western coast of India in the state of Gujarat, which was the most convenience point of landfall.

India embraced the new people as the Zoroastrians literally demonstrated to the Indians that they would melt into India as easily as sugar in warm milk. The Zoroastrians were made to feel welcome and became known as the Parsis because they were from the region of "Pars" in Iran (a region settled in the second millennium B.C. by migrants from Eastern Europe).

It is from these refugee immigrants that I have descended. Zoroastrians—also known as Parsis—adopted the rich and varied culture of Gujarat and eventually moved further south to Bombay. Parsis adopted the language of Gujarat and that is why Parsis speak Gujarati.

Moving forward, in the early 17th Century, the East India Company moved their headquarters to Bombay harbor after they leased the Seven Islands of Bombay from the British. Many Parsis who were living in the rural villages throughout the state of Gujarat and working for the East India Company also moved and started to find work in connection with the British government and public works.

The prolific migration from the villages in Gujarat and the outskirts of Bombay caused the wealthier Parsis of Bombay to fund trusts and erect trust buildings to house migrant workers. The trust buildings called were like college dormitories. Each floor had multiple single rooms and a common restroom.

The British soon recognized the Parsis as equals in the mercantile businesses. Soon, the Parsis dominated the brokerage houses where, as the principal merchants and ship-builders, they reigned foremost in the opium trade with China and engaged in philanthropy, fueled from their trade profits, throughout the city erecting educational, industrial and charitable entities. Some well-known Parsis include Zubin Mehta, Jamsetji Tata, Ratan Tata, and Persis Khambatta, even Freddy Mercury.

My culinary life began with my mother's influence of cooking every meal fresh with ingredients bought at the market that day. It was more of a necessity than a luxury and for several reasons. First, we could only afford a small fridge that was hardly spacious enough to hold more than bread, butter, some eggs, and a few sweet items. So, leftovers could not be stored.

Coomi Kolah, cooking in our home, 2016

Second, food was not preserved and mass produced due to the nationalistic attitude of the government after India's 1947 independence from the English. This attitude did not allow outside competition and thus a free market of products and services. Local vendors, locally grown and supplied foods, and home delivery of mainstays were the way things were done. Anything prepackaged, frozen, or coming from "abroad" was extremely expensive for the average person and was limited in supply due to nationalism. Only the very wealthy could afford "Western" foods via the black market.

Third, food was locally sourced and right from the farm, the chickens were cut in front of you at the market, the produce came from villages nearby on the morning trains, and grains were grown in the country, but rationed due to extreme government involvement in the market.

Storage of foods was almost impossible because nothing was preserved or treated with preservatives. In one day things would spoil. You ate only what you needed and bought again for the next day. Meal planning and procuring was a constant job.

My Culinary Kaleidoscope

A real culinary dish is a painting that the cook has crafted with the best ingredients and the intent to create. I have some vivid memories of my childhood that I cannot forget.

My parents, sister and I lived in a small room similar to a studio apartment. The entire living space was 200 square feet. Our beds were like day beds, with one trundle under the other that slept the four (4) of us, the shower was a stall that also functioned as the place to wash our dishes, there was a small sink next to the shower that was our washroom, and a small corner near the window had a shelf that held a small camping style gas stove.

It was in that tiny corner that my Mom created culinary memories. The space was small, but the warm loving childhood that my parents gave us created a place that we still love today. My parents refused to leave this loving home, my Mom still lives there.

When we awoke in the morning the first thing you were aware of was the aroma of the chai. The first thing people do in Bombay after brushing their teeth is to drink a cup of hot chai. On Saturday after our hot chai my Dad would take me to the market to buy fresh produce and meat.

As a child I showed a great interest in what to buy, determining which vendors were the most reliable and safe, and even how to bargain with the market vendors. At home I would watch my Mom clean and cut the meat and vegetables. She inspired and taught me so much about cooking. I would stand on a step-stool and insist on cooking by myself. My Dad was worried that I would get hurt cooking at such a young age, but my Mom would always encourage me to cook by using spices correctly, testing the meat for tenderness and cooking perfect rice without a cooker.

I entered catering college in Bombay and did my internship at the famous Taj Hotel. On the first day the chef gave me 50 pounds of onions to clean and cut, I was so scared and nervous, but I finished eight hours later. My experience at the Taj was amazing and I loved working in that big kitchen even though the training was difficult with many different shifts and no breaks.

Eventually I wanted to learn how to run a restaurant and I started working at a small restaurant called "Ideal Corner", which is famous for Parsi dishes and Indo-Chinese cuisine. I worked there for a few years until the owner wanted to retire and he offered me a job running the restaurants.

In 1987, I started running strictly vegetarian restaurants under Mr. Farhang Irani. He and I became very close as he took me under his wing and showed me everything about the business. I truly admired him. A few years later he opened a hotel and a non-vegetarian restaurant in Silvasa, a small village outside Bombay near the state of Gujarat. He sent me there to supervise. I learned how to manage a restaurant and hotel.

In 2000, I moved to the United States. Once here, I started working at a fast-food franchise in order to learn American business techniques and processes. I then took a position at an upscale Indian restaurant as a waiter so that I could experience first-hand about the American dining experience.

In 2004, I opened my first restaurant, Bombay Coast, in San Diego, California. I knew that the restaurant had to reflect the environment I grew up in near the coast and water. At that time, all the Indian restaurants were dark inside with blacked out windows and dim lighting. The ambiance was not Indian.

The dining experience should be more exact to what I had experienced in my Bombay—bright colors, open seating and spaces, patio dining and interaction with the staff. Californian tastes have allowed me to experiment with a cosmopolitan approach, like in Bombay. We have traditional Indian cuisine with a modern approach to today's diverse and experienced customer palate.

I introduced wraps, a bright and spicy cold salad and new curries. Some of the favorites are my creations of mango chicken masala, honey lemon chicken and sweet and spicy lamb shank.

In 2008, I opened another restaurant in the University of California at San Diego Price Center Food Court. To do this I had to submit a proposal for the restaurant to the University, it entailed an enormous amount of paperwork and two years of planning. There were several categories for the proposals and for ours, there were over thirty-five restaurants applying. Ultimately, Bombay Coast was selected.

It was thrilling to be selected and have the opportunity to become an ambassador of India, knowing that many students would now have an opportunity to try Indian cuisine. On average, Bombay Coast, UCSD serves five hundred meals a day.

Traditional Parsi dishes

 This Cookbook is not just a mere recitation of ingredients and a list of recipes. The reason I decided to write this book with my childhood and cultural recipes is to bring a bit of the wonderful creations that come about from various cultures mixing together. Life is a community endeavor, but appears very big from our individual perspectives.

 However, food is the universal truth because it links people, it bridges cultural differences, and it maintains its own integrity even when our political and social issues disintegrate. Food is truly life giving. Sharing recipes and the history in which they were created opens our minds and souls to a deeper human connection. That is what I can hopefully accomplish through this book of history, of food, and of sharing.

THE BASICS

Tandoor oven, making naan at restaurant

In this book I have tried to write some of the simpler recipes, easy for the beginner and classic for the experienced cook.

Cooking Times

Cooking times are determined on a gas range. Cooking can vary based on differing sizes and cuts of meat and fish. It is important to check that everything is cooked to your own personal satisfaction. There is one exception, and that is for chicken. Chicken should always be cooked all the way through.

There are rice recipes in this cookbook and some recipes that require cooked rice. If you are not comfortable cooking rice via a regular pot, then using a rice steamer is just fine. The rice steamers have pre-programmed times for the amount of rice that you want to cook or complex dishes that include rice.

Equipment

All the dishes in this book can be made in standard American pots, pans, and skillets. It does help, however, to use good quality heavy bottomed pots, especially for rice. When making Indian bread you can use a rounded griddle. For deep frying you can use a Chinese wok. Woks are readily available at standard retail housewares shop, specialty cooking and internet websites.

Tandoori Cooking

Even though the tikkas and naan are traditionally cooked in a tandoor oven, it is obvious that most people will not have a tandoor oven. Some might have a backyard pizza oven and that would be a great substitute for the tandoor oven. However, when making the recipes that require cooking in a Tandoor oven, the grill or convection oven will be fine to use.

The tandoor or clay pot oven originated in Persia and was brought to India via Afghanistan by traders. It is easy to understand the tandoor oven if one thinks of the Western brick oven. The clay is heated inside with wood or coal and the heat that cooks the meat or bread is live-fire, radiant heat and hot air revolving around the food. The food then gains a unique taste of the wood or coal and the earthen taste from the seasoned clay. Temperatures inside the oven can reach 900 degrees Fahrenheit, plus the oven stays hot for long periods.

Tandoor ovens are used in Southern, Central and Western Asia and many dishes can be cooked within them. For instance, all types of flatbread, seekh kebabs, stuffed naan, tandoori chicken (Punjabi), and chicken tikka (Mughlai) are some common examples.

Vendor selling differnt types of pulses: lentils, peas and beans

Choosing Ingredients

All cuisine depends on the quality of the ingredients used. Fresh vegetables, fruits, herbs and spices can be found in Indian grocery stores of major cities, or now, online. The more common spices can be found in supermarkets.

When the recipe calls for butter, you can choose salted or unsalted, but make sure that the butter is a whole butter and not margarine. Additionally, it is perfectly fine to substitute ghee for butter because ghee is a healthy fat. Remember, everything in moderation. Also, when using cooking oil, use high quality oil that has a higher burning point. Extra virgin olive oil is best when used for cooler temperatures or salads.

There are several recipes that include yogurt or cream. With those ingredients try to use whole and organic products, not non-fat or reduced fat because whole organic products do have the necessary healthy fats that our bodies need and being organic will help reduce the preservatives and chemicals that go into our bodies. Well sourced and wholesome foods do make a difference in our overall health and stays true to Bombay foods that are locally sourced and organic.

Bombay grocery store selling various lentils

Curry

In India, curry as the word is used today, simply means gravy. Indian curry, or gravy, is made by cooking the meat or vegetables along with lots of ingredients including whole milk, coconut milk, heavy cream, yogurt and a combination of spices. Traditionally, neither cornstarch nor flour is used to thicken the sauce to gravy.

Most curries start with the heating of cooking fat. Traditionally Indians prefer to use ghee, which is clarified butter, as it is more nutritious and gives a much richer, deeper flavor to the food. Ghee does indeed give a wonderful flavor, but, ghee can be substituted with any high temperature cooking oil that you prefer.

Tamarind

Tamarind is a type of a tree that is originally from Africa, but, because it does very well in tropical climates it can be found all over South Asia and Mexico. The name derives from Arabic Romanized tamar hindi, "Indian date". The pod that is grown from the tree is a legume that doesn't open naturally.

The seeds inside the pod are large and sticky, with a tart pulp and grow more tart as the seeds are dried. However, the more the pod is allowed to mature on the tree the sweeter the seeds and less acidic. Tamarind can be found at any Indian, Asian or South American store.

Today, India is the largest producer of tamarind and it is used in chutneys, basic dishes and desserts. Because the seed grows more tart as it is dried, a little goes a long way. To make it more palatable, sugar or honey dates are added to the pulped seed to use it as a base for chutneys, sauces, marinades and stews.

One more benefit of the tamarind seed is that it has the natural acidity needed to marinate and tenderize meat. In fact, tamarind seed pulp is used as one of the ingredients in Worcestershire sauce.

Tamarind

Saffron

Saffron is a spice that is harvested from the flower of the "saffron crocus", which is mainly grown from Spain in the West to India in the East. "Saffron" is an English term derived from the Latin word safranum via the 12-Century Old French term "safran" and "safranum" derives from the Persian term "za'feran". Saffron originated in West Asia and Persian Moguls brought it to India.

Saffron has been used as a medicine, as a perfume, as a dye and as a food enhancer. It can be used in savory and sweet dishes as its flavor is intense, thus, only a little is required for changing a good dish into a memorable one.

Saffron threads — $45 worth

In order to harvest the saffron, each worker must hand-pick the small stems of saffron from the flower, with just three stigmas per crocus flower. Half an ounce of saffron is more expensive than gold due its labor-intensive harvesting methods. About 200,000 delicate red strands of saffron must be hand-picked from 70,000 crocus sativa flowers to make 1 pound. The cost per kilo of saffron is about $2,000; or up to $315 an ounce or $5,000 a pound.

Buying Saffron: There are a few things you should be aware of when purchasing true saffron. Because of the high cost there are many counterfeit products on the market, here's what you should look for:

> **If there are long red threads**—this usually means that thread has been dyed;
>
> **A very uniform red color**—the threads have been dyed;
>
> **Streaks of yellow across the thread**—this occurs when saffron has been tinted, but a thread is covered by another, so the dye doesn't reach the thread below, leaving a red-yellow-red pattern.

There is one more thing to consider when using saffron—to use powder or threads. If you want more flexibility for your cooking, choose the threads. You can show off the threads in the dish and if you want, you can always pound the threads down to a powder. In all other aspects, both are equal.

Spices:

(Opposite page, from top left to right)

CINNAMON STICK
CARDAMON
CLOVE
CUMIN SEEDS
FENUGREEK LEAVES
DRIED RED CHILLIES
STAR ANISE
TURMERIC POWDER
CHILI POWDER
BAY LEAF

(On the right, from top to bottom)

GARAM MASALA
MUSTARD SEEDS
CORIANDER POWDER
BLACK PEPPERCORNS
NUTMEG

GARAM MASALA

INGREDIENTS

- 6 pods black cardamom
- 8 pods green cardamom
- 5 cinnamon sticks
- 16 cloves
- 5 teaspoons cumin seeds

METHOD

- On low heat, without oil or butter, lightly roast all ingredients on a griddle for 5 minutes, or just until lightly brown. Stir continuously and slowly.
- Once lightly brown, remove from heat and let cool.
- Once cool, grind to a fine powder in a blender/coffee grinder or using a mortar and pestle.
- Keep in an airtight container in dark storage.

GARLIC-GINGER PASTE

Garlic-ginger paste is specified in many of the recipes here and it can be time consuming to process every time. It is much easier to make the paste in large quantities, refrigerate and use as needed. The preparation method is the same for both ingredients. The paste can be stored in an airtight container or jar in the refrigerator for four to six weeks.

INGREDIENTS

- 8 cups fresh ginger, roughly chopped
- 8 cups fresh garlic cloves
- 1 cup water

METHOD

- Take the fresh ginger and the fresh garlic and soak both in separate containers overnight.
- After soaking, peel the garlic. Roughly chop the ginger.
- Place the peeled garlic without skin and ginger (skin on) in a food processor or blender.
- Add the water to start processing until the mix is pulped. Add half an ounce of water as necessary to get the right consistency. The right consistency is like watery paper pulp.
- Refrigerate the mix in an airtight container.

TANDOORI MASALA (POWDER)

MAKES: ½ cup

Tandoori Masala powder, aka, tandoor masala, is a mixture of spices used specifically for tandoor oven dishes, particularly tandoori chicken. The masala is usually applied to the meat along with yogurt. Tandoori masala is also used in dishes like tikka/butter chicken and in paneer tikka. You can make it yourself, or buy it ready-made from any Indian grocery store.

INGREDIENTS

- 2 teaspoons coriander seeds
- 2 teaspoons cumin seeds
- 1 teaspoon fenugreek seeds
- 1 teaspoon dried fenugreek leaves
- 1 teaspoon black peppercorns
- 1 teaspoon cloves
- 8 pieces black cardamom
- 2 teaspoons paprika
- 1 teaspoon ground cinnamon
- ½ teaspoon ground ginger
- ½ teaspoon chili powder

METHOD

- In a non-stick skillet on medium-low heat, roast all ingredients together, stirring constantly for 5-8 minutes. Stir carefully because as the spices cook they release their oils and brown, this makes them more pungent and that can be an irritant to the eyes and nose.

- After 5-8 minutes, take the spice mixture off the heat and let cool. Once cool, grind to a fine powder in a blender/coffee grinder.

- Store in an airtight container in a dark and dry storage.

APPETIZERS

ALOO PATTICE

CHICKEN LOLLIPOPS

EGGPLANT CUTLETS

ONION BHAJIAS (PAKODAS)

PANEER PAKODA

SAMOSAS—VEGETARIAN AND MEAT

PAPPADUM

RAISIN ALOO PANEER ROLLS

VEGGIE BALLS

Just like in any country, there are quick foods that start and become originals from the big cities to the rural towns and the micro-cultural nuances of each village. The best get passed on from generation to generation with little change and great back stories defining their beginnings.

In India, appetizers come from the North, the South, the East and the West. It is in the West that Bombay lies and it is here that indigenous foods married other visiting cultures on the shores of Bombay.

This section explores those appetizers—the Western origin of India blended with the visiting nations intertwined in Bombay.

Finger foods make an ideal start to the meal, without being too filling. In the restaurant, I serve our appetizers with mint chutney, tamarind chutney, spicy chutney, or mango chutney. A unique consideration for Indian appetizers is that the same appetizer can be made different ways depending on the region in which it is made.

ALOO PATTICE

MAKES: 10–12 pieces
PREPARATION: 20 minutes
COOKING: 20 minutes

Fried potato patty with spices

INGREDIENTS

- 4 Yukon gold potatoes—cooked and mashed
- 3 tablespoons green peas (fresh/frozen)—cooked and mashed
- ¼ cup of cilantro—chopped
- 2 green chillies—minced
- 1 ½ tablespoons cumin powder
- 1 teaspoon dry mango powder (available in Indian grocery store)
- Quality frying oil
- Salt to taste

METHOD

- In a large bowl, add the mashed potatoes, green chillies, cilantro, cumin powder, mashed green peas, mango powder and salt. Mix well. Then, using your hands, shape the potato mixture into moon shape pudgy cakes.

- In a shallow frying pan, heat the frying oil to medium-high and carefully fry each potato patty until golden brown all over. Turn each cake often so that one side doesn't get over-done. Once fried, take each out and place on paper towels to soak up any excess oil.

- Serve with channa masala.

CHICKEN LOLLIPOPS

SERVES: 6–8
PREPARATION: 4 hours marination; 40 minutes thereafter
COOKING: 20 minutes

A delicious snack made from chicken wings and resembles lollipops

INGREDIENTS

- 2 pounds plain chicken wings
- ½ red onion—sliced in half circles or rings (your preference)
- 2 teaspoons garlic-ginger paste
- 2 teaspoons chili powder
- 4 tablespoons cake flour or all-purpose Indian flour (Maida—available in Indian grocery store)
- 1 teaspoon garam masala
- 1 teaspoon tandoori masala
- 5-6 lemon wedges
- Quality frying oil
- Salt to taste

METHOD

- Take each chicken wing and cut it into three pieces according to the joints of the wings. Chop the wing at the joints and don't use the pointy end. Using the largest piece, cut the chicken away from the bone (like a crown of lamb) at the fat end. Using your fingers, push the meat down to the end.

- In a bowl, place the chicken wings, garlic-ginger paste, chili powder, garam masala, tandoori masala and salt. Mix well and let them marinate in the refrigerator for 4 hours.

- In a frying pan, heat oil to medium-high. Gently coat each chicken lollipop in the flour and drop into the hot oil. Fry until done. When done place the lollipops on paper towels to absorb any excess oil. Wrap each end with foil in order to hold while eating.

- Serve the lollipops on the onion slices with the lemon wedges.

EGGPLANT CUTLETS

SERVES: 4–6
PREPARATION: 30 minutes for soaking; 15 minutes thereafter
COOKING: 20 minutes

Spiced fried eggplant cutlets

INGREDIENTS

- 2 large eggplants—sliced
- 2 tablespoons white vinegar
- 1 tablespoon kosher or sea salt
- ½ teaspoon chili powder
- ½ teaspoon paprika powder
- ¼ teaspoon turmeric powder
- ¼ teaspoon garam masala
- Bread crumbs
- Quality frying oil
- 1 teaspoon salt to taste

METHOD

- Skin and slice the eggplant into round slices, about ½ inch thick. Prick each slice with a fork. Mix the salt and vinegar together to make a paste. Then rub each side of the eggplant slices with the salt-vinegar paste. Let the slices sit for 30 minutes. After 30 minutes remove the slices and shake off any excess water. The salt absorbs the eggplant's bitterness.

- In a bowl, mix the chili powder, paprika powder, turmeric powder, and garam masala with a little water. Apply this mix to both sides of the slices. Coat the eggplant slices with bread crumbs and arrange on a plate.

- In a frying pan, heat the oil to medium-high heat. As soon as the oil begins to smoke, take each slice separately and fry in batches of 4-6 depending upon the size of your frying pan.

- Brown each side (approximately 2 minutes each side) and remove from the pan once done. Place the slices on a paper towel in order to absorb any excess oil.

- Serve warm with tamarind chutney.

ONION BHAJIAS (PAKODAS)

SERVES: 8–10 people
COOKING: 10 minutes
PREPARATION: 8 minutes

During monsoon season, days are filled with rain, most often lasting days without a break. We used to ask my Mom to make some hot Bhajias on rainy days because everything was flooded and there was nowhere to go.

Bhajias are a classic snack of India, they are like onion fritters. So, within 10 minutes my Mom had them hot and ready for us to enjoy with our fresh tamarind chutney and chai.

INGREDIENTS

- 2 cups gram flour (Besan—available in Indian grocery store)
- 2 large yellow onions—sliced
- 2 green chillies—minced
- 2 bunches cilantro—chopped
- 1 teaspoon baking powder
- ½ teaspoon chili powder
- ½ teaspoon turmeric
- ½ teaspoon cumin seed/onion seeds
- Quality frying oil
- Salt to taste
- Water as needed to thicken batter

METHOD

- In a mixing bowl, add gram flour, chili powder, turmeric powder, onions, baking powder, cumin seeds, onion, seeds, green chillies, cilantro and salt. Mix well and add water to adjust the batter. The batter should be thick like a fritter batter, but, not so thick as to form a dry paste.

- In a deep frying pan, heat oil to medium-high heat and place a spoonful size portion of the batter into the oil. Be careful to place and not drop the batter as you don't want any oil to splatter up.

- Fry small batches at a time as the batter makes the oil dirty, will cool off the oil and give the bhajias a burnt flavor. As you are frying, roll each bhajia around so that all sides are fried to a golden brown. You want to make sure the gram flour batter is thoroughly cooked. Once done, remove each bhajia and set on paper towels to absorb any excess oil.

- Serve hot with mint and tamarind chutney.

PANEER PAKODA

SERVES: 5
PREPARATION: 10 minutes
COOKING: 20 minutes

Fried cheese made with chickpea flour

INGREDIENTS

- 1 package Paneer (available in Indian grocery store; or make your own using the Paneer recipe on pg. 132)
- 1 cup besan (gram flour)
- 2 pinches baking powder
- ½ teaspoon chaat masala* (available in Indian grocery store)
- 2 teaspoons chili powder
- 1 teaspoon garam masala
- 1 teaspoon coriander powder
- 1 cup water
- Quality frying oil
- Salt to taste

* Chaat masala is a spice powder mix that contains dried mango powder, cumin, coriander, dried ginger, salt, black pepper, asafetida and chili powder.

METHOD

- In a mixing bowl, add besan (gram) flour, baking powder, chili powder, garam masala, coriander powder, salt and water. Mix well. The mix should be like a thick pancake batter not thick like a paste. Add water as needed, start with ½ cup.

- Cut paneer into 1 ½ inch squares which are slightly thicker than ¼ inch thickness.

- In a deep pot/frying pan, heat the oil to medium-high. Once hot, gently slide in each coated paneer piece. Do not fry too many at time as the batter will cool the oil down and unnecessarily dirty the oil. Fry all sides until they are golden brown. Once done, remove the paneer and place on paper towels in order to absorb the excess oil.

- While they are hot, sprinkle the chaat masala over them and serve with mint and tamarind, and spicy chutneys.

PAPPADUMS

Pappadums are seasoned black gram flour crisps. Other flours that pappadums are made from include lentils, chickpeas, rice, tapioca or potato. The kneaded dough is flattened into thin rounds and then air-dried.

INGREDIENTS

Uncooked pappadum is easily found in any Indian market. There are many varieties. Some are without any spice, and some have a variety of spices. It is really a matter of taste and to try out the different varieties to find out which is best for you. However, one needs to fry or bake them before serving.

- Kitchen tongs.

METHOD

- **TEMPERATURE OF OIL**: If the oil is not hot enough the pappadum will not expand immediately once placed in the oil. If the oil is too hot, then the pappadum will begin to brown. Turn down the heat. The pappadum should retain their yellow color.

- **FRYING**: In a skillet, heat oil to medium-hot. When hot, put in 1 pappadum, it should sizzle and expand immediately. Then turn it over and leave for a few seconds then remove. Place the cooked pappadum on paper towels to absorb any excess oil.

- **ROASTING**: This is the easiest method of cooking the pappadum and is very quick. Here, you will want to roast over an open flame and the source can be charcoal, a propane grill, a camping stove, a kitchen blow torch (like those used for crème brule). Take the pappadum in the tongs and hold over the flame until it starts crisping. Then turn over and over until the entire pappadum is cooked. Remember it cooks very fast, so don't hold it over the flame for longer than a couple of seconds at time.

- Serve immediately with chutneys. Pappadum has a tendency to get soft when left to sit after frying. So, serve as soon as you fry them.

RAISIN ALOO PANEER ROLLS

SERVES: 4–6
PREPARATION: 30 minutes
COOKING: 20 minutes

Savory fried potato rolls with cheese, raisins and herbs

INGREDIENTS

- 4 Yukon gold potatoes- cooked and mashed
- ½ pound paneer—crumbled (ready-made paneer available in Indian grocery store; or use the Paneer recipe on pg. 132)
- 5 tablespoons Maida flour (cake flour) or tempura mix
- ½ cup dry bread crumbs
- 2 tablespoons golden raisins
- ½ teaspoon chili powder
- ½ teaspoon turmeric powder
- 1 bunch cilantro—chopped
- 1 tablespoon unsalted butter
- ½ cup organic whole milk
- Quality frying oil
- Salt to taste

METHOD

- Golden raisins are usually plump so they don't need soaking. If you are using the darker raisin, then soak them for 30 minutes in warm water.
- In a mixing bowl, add the mashed potatoes, paneer, chili powder, turmeric powder, cilantro, raisins, and salt. Mix well.
- Form 6-7 rolls from the mixture. The rolls should have the shape of a thick stubby cigar.
- Take the Maida flour or tempura mix and place it in a flat pan or dish. Lightly dust each roll in the flour/tempura mix and then roll each firmly in the bread crumbs to coat well. Gently dip the roll in the milk and then roll again in the bread crumbs firmly coating all sides.
- In a deep pan, heat the frying oil to medium-high and gently fry each roll. Turn them after each side becomes a golden brown, making sure all sides are cooked. After done, place the cooked rolls on paper towels in order to soak up any excess oil.
- Serve them with ketchup or any sweet chutney.

SAMOSAS (VEGETABLE OR MEAT)

MAKES: 8–10 pieces
PREPARATION: 40 minutes
COOKING: 10–15 minutes

Crisp turnover filled with potatoes, green peas and spices. For meat samosa, see the recipe of Kheema Curry recipe on pg. 204, but, make it dry and use the kheema to fill in the pocket of pastry.

INGREDIENTS

- ¾ cup plain flour
  (Maida—available in Indian grocery store)
- ¼ cup semolina (Suji)
- ¼ teaspoon baking powder
- ¼ teaspoon salt
- 1 large yellow potato—
  cooked and coarsely mashed
- 2 tablespoons cilantro—chopped
- ½ teaspoon red chili powder
- ½ teaspoon cumin powder
- 1 teaspoon cumin seeds/ mustard seeds
- 1 tablespoon quality cooking oil
- Quality frying oil
- Salt to taste

METHOD

- Sift flour, semolina, salt and baking powder into a bowl. Add 1 tablespoon of oil and water to form firm dough—add water as necessary. Knead for 5-8 minutes until dough becomes smooth and elastic. Cover the dough and set aside for 30 minutes.
- **FILLING**: Heat 2 tablespoons of oil in a frying pan on very low heat. Add cumin seeds, mustard seeds, chili powder, and salt. Cook for a 30 seconds. In a bowl, add the mashed potato and the cooked spices. Mix well.
- From the dough make small golf ball sized rounds. Take each round and then cut them in half to make a half-moon shape. Brush some water on the edge of the half-moon piece. Pick up the half circle and roll into a cone shape, pressing firmly to seal the seam. Fill cone with 1 tablespoon of filling. Then take the top open flap sides and press together like sealing lips together with your fingers.
- Heat frying oil on medium-high to high. Fry the samosas in small batches until they are golden brown all over.
- Serve with tamarind chutney and mint chutney.

VEGGIE BALLS

SERVES: 8–10
PREPARATION: 20 minutes
COOKING: 10–15 minutes

Mixed vegetable kebabs with herbs and spices

INGREDIENTS

- ½ cup semolina flour (Suji)
- 1 cup whole organic milk
- Mixed vegetables: 4-6 green beans, 1 carrot, and ¼ cabbage—diced
- ¼ cup cilantro—chopped
- 1 cup Paneer cheese (available in any Indian grocery store; or use the Paneer recipe on pg. 132)—crumbled
- ½ cup plain bread crumbs
- 1 teaspoon tomato sauce
- ¼ teaspoon garam masala
- ½ teaspoon red chili powder
- ½ teaspoon chaat masala
- 2 teaspoons fresh lemon juice
- 1 tablespoon unsalted butter
- Quality frying oil
- Salt to taste

METHOD

- In a pan, heat the butter over medium heat. Add diced carrots and beans, salt to taste and sauté for 3 minutes. Add cabbage and sauté for another 5 minutes. Turn the heat to low and cover the pan. Cook until the vegetables are soft. Once soft, remove the vegetables from the pan and set aside. In the same pan, on low heat, add semolina (suji) and stir fry for 2-3 minutes.

- Then, after 3 minutes, add milk and stir continuously until thick. Once thick, add the paneer and cilantro and stir well for 30 seconds.

- After 30 seconds remove the semolina mixture from the heat and transfer to a bowl. Add the garam masala, chili powder, chaat masala, lemon juice, tomato sauce and sauted vegetables. Mix well. Add salt to taste. Once mixed, form round patty shapes and set them aside in a plate.

- In a frying pan, heat oil to medium-high and carefully drop each patty into the oil. To make crisper balls, keep the balls in a freezer for 15-30 minutes before frying. Fry the balls until golden brown. When done, place the balls on paper towels to absorb the excess oil.

- Serve warm with mint chutney.

MEAT RECIPES

(Lamb—Memana; Chicken—Murgh)

LAMB RECIPES

LAMB CHOP	LAMB SEEKH KEBAB
LAMB CURRY	LAMB SHANK
LAMB KATHI ROLL	KASHMIRI LAMB ROGAN JOSH

CHICKEN RECIPES

ACHARI MURGH

BALTI CHICKEN PASANDA

CHICKEN CURRY

CHICKEN KORMA

CHICKEN TIKKA KEBAB

CHICKEN TIKKA MASALA

CHICKEN VINDALOO

DRY JEERA CHICKEN

EAST INDIAN CHICKEN CURRY

GARLIC CHICKEN DRY

HONEY LEMON CHICKEN

KARAHI (WOK) CHICKEN

MANGO CHICKEN MASALA

METHI MURGH

MURGH MUSSALAM

RED-GOLD SAFFRON CHICKEN

RESHMI KEBAB (SILKEN KEBAB)

TANDOORI CHICKEN

LAMB CHOP

SERVES: 4–6

PREPARATION: Overnight marination, or at least 1 hour; then 15 minutes remaining preparation.

COOKING: 50 minutes

Lamb chop grilled with dry masala

INGREDIENTS

- 1-2 pounds lamb chops
- ¾ cup yogurt
- 2 teaspoons garlic–ginger paste
- 1 teaspoon chili powder
- 2 teaspoons coriander powder
- ½ teaspoon turmeric powder
- 1 teaspoon garam masala
- 1 teaspoon malt vinegar
- 2 tablespoons extra virgin olive oil
- 2 tablespoons unsalted butter
- Salt to taste

METHOD

- In a bowl, marinate lamb chops with yogurt, garlic-ginger paste, chili powder, coriander powder, turmeric powder, garam masala, malt vinegar and salt. Let it marinate for at least one hour, preferably overnight.

- After the lamb chops marinate, add the olive oil to the lamb chops and mix well. Once mixed, remove the lamb chops from the marinade and let them sit to room temperature for 30 minutes.

- While the lamb chops sit at room temperature heat a grill or barbeque to medium-high heat. Once to temperature, place the lamb chops on the grill/barbeque and grill them on each side, making sure both sides are uniformly brown. Brush both sides with a little melted butter. Grill each side for two minutes to reach a medium-rare.

- Once to your desired temperature, remove from the grill and let them sit for 1 minute. Serve with mint chutney, sliced red onions and lime wedges.

LAMB CURRY

SERVES: 4
PREPARATION: 30 minutes
COOKING: 1 ½ hours

Boneless lamb cooked with tomatoes and chillies

INGREDIENTS

- 2 pounds boneless lamb—cut into bite sized chunks
- 4 large yellow onions—diced
- 4 large tomatoes—diced
- 3 ½ ounces garlic-ginger paste
- ¾ teaspoon red chili paste
- 10 pieces clove
- 8 pieces green cardamom
- 1 ½ cups quality cooking oil
- 2 teaspoons salt
- Fresh cilantro for garnish

METHOD

- In a large pot, heat ½ cup of oil in a pot over medium-high heat and add the onions. Fry the onions until just golden brown. This process lets out the onions' natural sugars and they caramelize.

- Then add the garlic-ginger paste, all 8 pieces of green cardamom and the 10 pieces of cloves to the pot of onions. Stir for 30 seconds. Add the boneless lamb to the pot, mixing well with the other ingredients. Allow the lamb to simmer on low heat until the oil rises to the surface above the curry gravy.

- Then add the salt. Stir well, and then add water as desired for dry or wet curry. Cook covered on very low heat until the lamb is tender.

- Adjust the seasoning per taste.

- Garnish with cilantro just before serving.

- **REMEMBER:** When garnishing with cilantro, wait until right before serving to put it on the food, otherwise it wilts and becomes soggy.

LAMB KATHI ROLL

SERVES: 8–10
PREPARATION: Overnight marination; then 15 minutes remaining preparation.
COOKING: 40–50 minutes

Skewer-roasted kebab wrapped in paratha

INGREDIENTS

- 4 pounds boneless leg of lamb—cut into small chunks
- 1 cup of yogurt
- 9 cloves garlic—diced
- 2 tablespoons garlic-ginger paste
- 3 teaspoons ground cumin powder
- 1 teaspoon chili powder
- 1 teaspoon black pepper
- ¼ cup orange juice
- ¼ cup extra virgin olive oil
- Mint chutney
  (see mint chutney recipe on pg. 229; can buy ready-made in Indian grocery store)
- Tamarind chutney
  (see tamarind chutney recipe on pg. 233; can buy ready-made in Indian grocery store)
- Paratha
  (see Paratha recipe on pg. 183; can buy ready-made in Indian grocery store)
- Salt to taste

METHOD

- On a baking sheet lay out the chunks of lamb.
- In a small bowl, whisk the yogurt with the oil, garlic, garlic-ginger paste, cumin powder, chili powder, black pepper, salt and orange juice. Mix well. Then, rub this mix all over the lamb. Leave the lamb in the bowl of marinade. Wrap the bowl in plastic, place the lamb and marinade in an airtight bowl and refrigerate overnight.
- Preheat the oven to 450 degrees. Lay the lamb on a rack set over a baking sheet, cover and let rest for 30 minutes at room temperature.
- After resting for 30 minutes, roast the lamb for 30-35 minutes.
- Check the meat with a thermometer inserted in the center of a cube; medium-rare will register 130 degrees. Cook the lamb to well-done.
- Take it out of the oven and let it rest for 15 minutes. Then thinly slice the lamb and serve over hot parathas, add mint chutney, tamarind chutney, sliced onions and lime.

LAMB SEEKH KEBAB

SERVES: 6
PREPARATION: Overnight marination; thereafter 20 minutes preparation.
COOKING: 30–50 minutes

Minced lamb skewer

INGREDIENTS

- 6-8 metal or wooden skewers. Before using wooden skewers always soak them in water overnight, otherwise they splinter.
  NOTE: If you are using a tandoor oven, DO NOT use wooden skewers—the intense heat will burn the skewers, instead use metal skewers.

- 1 pound minced lamb
- 1 teaspoon garam masala
- 3 teaspoons gram flour (garbanzo bean/chickpea flour—can be found in Indian grocery stores)
- 1 cup onion paste*
- 1 ½ tablespoons garlic-ginger paste
- 1 teaspoon chili powder
- 1 teaspoon nutmeg
- 1 teaspoon cinnamon powder
- ½ cup cilantro—chopped
- 4 teaspoons oil— to include in the mix
- Salt to taste
- Olive oil for brushing of skewers

METHOD

* Onion paste:
  - 1 large yellow onion—quartered
  - 1 cup water
  - In a small saucepan, combine 1 large yellow onion and water, bring to a boil, then simmer over low heat until the onion is just tender—about 20 minutes. Transfer the onion to a blender/processor and puree.

- In a large bowl, mix all the ingredients thoroughly with the lamb.
- Marinate overnight in a covered container in the refrigerator.
- With greased hands make long sausage shaped kebabs and mold it around the skewers evenly.
- Brush the skewers with good extra virgin olive oil and grill in a tandoor oven, or over a grill turning them to achieve a uniform browning.
- Serve preferably with mint and tamarind chutneys, or mango chutney, and lemon slices.

LAMB SHANK

SERVES: 3
PREPARATION: 25 minutes
COOKING: 4 hours

Slow cooked leg of lamb

INGREDIENTS

- 2 lamb shanks
- 2 ½ cups yellow onions—diced
- 1 large tomato—chopped
- 3 teaspoons garlic-ginger paste
- 3 ½ cups yogurt
- 1 ½ teaspoons garam masala
- 1 ½ teaspoons cumin seeds
- 1 ½ teaspoons coriander seeds
- 1 cup of quality cooking oil
- Salt to taste
- Fresh cilantro for garnish

METHOD

- Heat the oil in a wok or deep cooking pot over medium-high, then add the onions and cook until golden brown. Add the lamb shanks and seer each side for 3 minutes. Add the garam masala, cumin seeds, coriander seeds, chopped tomato, garlic-ginger paste and sauté for 5 minutes. Then, add enough hot water to cover the shank and bring to a boil. Cover with a lid and simmer 3-4 hours, or until done.

- Remove the shanks and set aside. Strain the cooking liquid into a separate pot and cook for another 10 minutes or until reduced to the desired consistency.

- Add the shanks back to the reduced liquid cover and simmer for 15 minutes.

- Garnish with cilantro.

Rogan (roughan) means "clarified butter/fat", and josh (jus) means "intensity"/"passion". Rogan josh is a staple of Kashmiri cuisine and part of the multi-course meal called the "Wazwan". The dish was brought to Kashmir by the Mugals.

KASHMIRI LAMB ROGAN JOSH

SERVES: 6–8
PREPARATION: 50 minutes
COOKING: 1 ½-2 hours

Rich tomato based lamb stew (no onion recipe)

INGREDIENTS

- 3 pounds boneless lamb cut into bite sized pieces
- 4 tablespoons plain yogurt
- 3 tablespoons tomato puree
- 2 teaspoons whole organic milk (warm)
- 1 teaspoon granulated sugar
- 1 ½ cups water
- 4 tablespoons extra virgin olive oil
- 1 teaspoon butter
- 2 pieces star anise
- 3 cinnamon sticks
- 2 bay leaves
- ½ teaspoon cardamom powder
- 2 teaspoons chili powder
- 2 teaspoons fennel seeds
- 2 teaspoons cumin seeds
- 2 teaspoons garam masala
- 3 cloves
- Pinch of nutmeg
- 4-5 pieces saffron threads
- Salt to taste

METHOD

- Put the lamb in a large bowl and mix in the yogurt, salt and bay leaves and set aside for 30 minutes.
- Take the saffron threads and soak them in warm milk and set aside.
- Heat the cooking oil in a heavy based sauce pan over medium-high heat, when the oil is hot, add the nutmeg, the star anise and fry for 1 minute, stirring constantly. After 1 minute, add the lamb.
- Turn the lamb pieces over in the oil several times and cook for 2 minutes to seal the juices inside and sear the pieces all over.
- After 2 minutes, cover and simmer the lamb in its own juices. Add 2-3 ounces of water if needed to cook further in order to make the meat tender.
- Make a well in the center of the pot with the lamb and add the sugar with butter, tomato puree, cardamom powder, cloves, chili powder, fennel seeds, cumin seeds, and garam masala.
- Cook and stir frequently for a further 10 to 20 minutes or until the oil separates from the lamb curry.
- To finish, drizzle with the entire saffron milk and serve hot with rice or naan.

ACHARI MURGH

SERVES: 5
PREPARATION: 25 minutes
COOKING: 40–45 minutes

Pickled chicken

INGREDIENTS

- 2 pounds skinless, boneless chicken breast—cut into 2 inch pieces
- 2 large yellow onions—sliced
- 7 ounces plain whole yogurt
- 1 teaspoon fenugreek seeds
- 5 teaspoons garlic-ginger paste
- 1 teaspoon red chili powder
- 1 teaspoon coriander powder
- 2 teaspoons fresh lemon juice
- ¼ cup cilantro—chopped
- 1¼ cup of quality cooking oil
- 1 cup water
- Salt to taste

For the ACHARI spices (masala)—mix together and set aside

- 1 ½ teaspoon onion seeds
- 2 teaspoons anise seed (saunf)
- 2 ½ teaspoons cumin seeds
- 5 whole red chillies

METHOD

- Heat a pan on medium-high heat, add the sliced onions and achari spices. Sauté until onions are golden brown. Then add the fenugreek seeds. Cook for 1 minute.

- Add the garlic-ginger paste, red chili, turmeric, coriander and yogurt. Cook until the oil rises to the surface.

- Add the chicken, stir for 5 minutes, then add 1 cup of water and salt to taste. Cook on low heat until the water reduces and the chicken becomes tender.

- Add the lemon juice and stir.

- Serve hot garnished with cilantro.

BALTI CHICKEN PASANDA

SERVES: 6
PREPARATION: 2 hours marination; 30 minutes thereafter
COOKING: 1 hour

Thick, creamy gravy with chicken

"Pasanda" is Urdu for "favorite" and is a popular North Indian dish derived from the Mughal Emperors. Any prime cut of meat will work with this dish. One may also use king prawns.

INGREDIENTS

- 1 ½ pounds skinless, boneless chicken breast—cubed
- 4 tablespoons Greek style yogurt
- 2 large yellow onions—diced
- 4 ½ cups heavy cream
- 1 teaspoon garlic-ginger paste
- 2 green chillies—chopped
- ½ teaspoon cumin seeds
- 2 teaspoons cardamom powder
- 1 teaspoon black pepper—ground
- 2 teaspoons garam masala
- 2 cinnamon sticks
- 1 tablespoon ground almonds
- 1 teaspoon chili powder
- 2 green chillies—diced
- 2 tablespoons cilantro—chopped
- 5 tablespoons quality cooking oil

METHOD

- Mix the yogurt, cumin seeds, cardamom, black pepper, garam masala, ground almonds, garlic-ginger paste, chili powder and salt in a medium mixing bowl. Add the chicken pieces and leave to marinate for about 2 hours.

- In a large pan, heat the cooking oil over medium-high heat and cook the onions until golden brown/translucent.

- Once translucent, add the marinated chicken and stir well. Cook for 5 minutes and then add the cinnamon sticks. Cook on a medium heat for 12-15 minutes or until the sauce thickens and the chicken is tender.

- Add the green chillies, cilantro and pour in the heavy cream, bring the mixture to a boil, then reduce the heat and simmer for another 10 minutes.

- Serve with parathas.

CHICKEN CURRY

SERVES: 6
PREPARATION: 20 minutes
COOKING: 30–35 minutes

Boneless chicken cooked in a medium spicy curry

INGREDIENTS

- 2 pounds boneless chicken—cut in ½ inch pieces
- 2 large yellow onions—blended to a puree
- 2 large tomatoes—blended to a puree
- 2 pieces green chili—diced
- 4 curry leaves (available in Indian grocery store)
- ½ teaspoon cinnamon powder
- 1 teaspoon cumin seeds
- 2 cardamom pods
- 2 cinnamon sticks
- 3 cloves
- 1 teaspoon chili powder
- 1 teaspoon coriander powder
- 1 teaspoon turmeric powder
- ½ teaspoon garam masala
- ½ teaspoon cumin powder
- 2 teaspoons coconut powder
- 1 cup water
- 2 teaspoons quality cooking oil
- Salt to taste

METHOD

- Heat the oil in a pan over medium heat. When hot, add cumin seeds, cardamom, curry leaves, cinnamon stick and the cloves and fry for 30 seconds. Be careful as adding spices to hot oil tends to cause the spices to pop like popcorn and release their oils. Add them carefully.

- Carefully add the chicken pieces and ½ cup water, cover and cook the chicken, stirring occasionally for 10-20 minutes. Cook chicken until golden brown.

- In a separate pan, add 1 tablespoon of oil and heat to medium-high heat, grill the onions until golden brown and then add them to the blender and puree. Be careful as the onions are hot and they will splatter in the blender. Be sure to cover the blender when you blend them. Once pureed, set aside.

- In the same pan, add ½ tablespoon of oil and cook the tomatoes down a bit, about 3-5 minutes, then add them to the blender and puree. Add the onions to the tomato puree and blend together.

- In the pot with the chicken, add the onion-tomato puree, green chilis, cinnamon powder, coriander powder, turmeric powder, cumin powder, coconut powder, and salt to taste to the chicken and cook for another 10 minutes on low heat. Stir regularly.

- Finish with a sprinkling of fresh cilantro and serve with Basmati rice.

The word "curry" derives from the Tamil word "kari" or "spiced sauce"; as India gave way to Portuguese and British rule, the term "curry" became synonymous with any Indian sauce to go with rice. And as the Portuguese introduced Mexican and South American chillies to India, curry became more spicy.

CHICKEN KORMA

SERVES: 4
PREPARATION: 25 minutes
COOKING: 40 minutes

Boneless white meat chicken cooked in a mild coconut curry.

"Korma" is derived from Urdu meaning "braise", and has its roots in the Mughlai cuisine of 16th Century India.

INGREDIENTS

- 8 pieces chicken drumsticks
- 2 large yellow onions—chopped
- ¾ cup plain whole yogurt (preferably cream top)
- 1 bunch cilantro—chopped
- 3 tablespoons coconut powder
- 2 slices of fresh ginger root
- 2 tablespoons garlic-ginger paste
- 1 tablespoon cashew nuts
- ½ tablespoon turmeric powder
- 1 tablespoon red chili powder
- ¾ cup water
- 5 tablespoons quality cooking oil
- Salt to taste

METHOD

- Grind the onions, cashew nuts, and coconut powder with ¼ cup yogurt and ¼ cup water to form a smooth paste and set aside.

- Heat oil on medium-high heat in a pan, add garlic-ginger paste and stir well, then add the chicken and let it cook for about 2-3 minutes. Keep stirring. Once the chicken becomes brown, add turmeric, chili powder, and the paste made above. Simmer and stir occasionally until the gravy thickens.

- Add salt to taste.

- Add chopped cilantro and serve with Basmati rice.

DRY JEERA CHICKEN

SERVES: 6
PREPARATION: 20 minutes
COOKING: 35–40 minutes

Boneless chicken cooked with cumin seeds

INGREDIENTS

- 1 pound skinless, boneless chicken breast—cut into 1 inch pieces
- 1 bunch cilantro—chopped
- 3 tablespoons cumin seeds
- 1 tablespoon coriander seeds
- 1 teaspoon ground cumin
- ½ teaspoon cardamom powder
- ½ teaspoon black peppercorns—ground
- 1 small piece ginger—sliced
- 1 teaspoon garlic-ginger paste
- 4 green chillies—finely chopped
- 1 teaspoon garam masala
- 3 tablespoons quality cooking oil
- 1 cup water
- Salt to taste

METHOD

- Dry roast the coriander seeds and ½ tablespoon cumin seeds in a frying pan on high heat for about 30 seconds. Stir constantly and carefully. After 30 seconds, transfer to a small bowl, let cool, grind, and set aside.

- Heat the oil in a heavy pan over medium heat, add the cardamom powder, black pepper, and the remaining 2 ½ tablespoons cumin seeds, then fry for about 30 seconds until the seeds begin to sizzle. Stir constantly and carefully.

- Add the ginger, garlic-ginger paste, the roasted coriander/cumin mix (made above), cumin powder, and some salt to taste. Fry for 2 minutes and then add the chicken and chopped green chillies. Cook for 5 minutes, stirring constantly. Thereafter, add the garam masala and add the water, then cover and simmer for 20-30 minutes.

- Cook on low heat until the water is reduced and the chicken is tender, and dry.

- Garnish with the cilantro and serve.

CHICKEN TIKKA KEBAB

SERVES: 4
PREPARATION: 90 minutes combined marination; 10 minutes thereafter
COOKING: 30 minutes

Chicken tikka, also known as Murgh tikka, is small pieces of boneless chicken baked using skewers in the tandoor oven. Tikka means "bits"/"pieces".

INGREDIENTS

- 2 pounds skinless, boneless chicken breast—cubed
- 2 large red onions—cut into squares
- 1 green, red, yellow bell peppers—cut into squares
- ¼ cup fresh lemon juice
- ¼ cup yogurt
- 4 tablespoons tandoori masala (see tandoori masala recipe on pg. 26; also available in any Indian grocery store)
- 2 tablespoons butter
- Salt to taste
- 6-8 inch bamboo skewers soaked in water for 30 minutes (12 pieces)

METHOD

- Cut chicken breast into 1 inch pieces and combine with lemon juice and salt in a bowl. Cover and let stand for 30 minutes.
- After 30 minutes, add yogurt and tandoori masala to the chicken, cover and put in the refrigerator for 1 hour.
- After 1 hour, take chicken pieces and thread 1 piece of chicken, 1 piece of onion and 1 piece of bell pepper on to a skewer, do this for each skewer until pieces are used. Spread the remaining marinade on the chicken only.
- Apply butter with brush on both sides of the skewers and roast over a barbeque grill until chicken is cooked thoroughly—juices run clear.
- Serve hot with mint chutney.

This is a favorite at my restaurants. At UCSD we sell almost 80 pounds a day of chicken tikka masala. Various stories of the origin of Chicken Tikka Masala state that it originated in British India and has become England's national dish.

CHICKEN TIKKA MASALA

SERVES: 6
PREPARATION: 40–50 minutes
COOKING: 45 minutes–1 hour

Boneless tandoori chicken in a mild creamy curry

INGREDIENTS

- 15 pieces chicken tikka kebabs (see chicken tikka kebab recipe pg. 76)
- 3 large tomatoes—pureed
- 3 large yellow onions—sliced, fried and then pureed
- ½ cup cashew nuts (soaked in hot water for 15 minutes)
- 1-1 ½ cups whole organic milk
- ½ cup heavy cream
- 2 teaspoons garlic-ginger paste
- 1 teaspoon paprika powder
- 1 teaspoon garam masala
- 1 teaspoon sugar
- 1 teaspoon tandoor masala (available in Indian grocery store; or use recipe on pg. 26)
- 3 bay leaves
- 4 teaspoons unsalted butter
- Salt to taste
- Chopped cilantro for garnish

METHOD

- Soak cashews in hot water for 15 minutes, drain and grind to a very fine paste with a little water.
- In a pan over medium-high heat, add the sliced onions and cook them until golden brown to translucent. Then, remove them from the heat, let them cool and add them to a blender. Blend them to a puree. Then add the cashew puree to onion puree and mix together.
- Melt the butter in a pan over medium heat, then add a bay leaf and garlic-ginger paste and cook until the liquid evaporates and the paste turns a bit of a golden brown color.
- Then add the tomato puree, cashew and onion paste and stir for a few seconds. Add the paprika powder, garam masala, tandoori masala, salt and sugar. Cook until the mixture becomes dry and the fat separates from the mixture.
- Then, add milk, cream and enough water (about 1 cup) to get a thick curry. Mix well, bring to a boil, stirring constantly. Once the gravy starts to boil, cover and turn the heat down to a simmer for 10 minutes until the gravy turns to a bright red color and the fat surfaces.
- Add tandoori chicken pieces and simmer on low heat for 5 minutes (since the tandoori chicken pieces are already cooked, all that remains is to simmer together for the 5 minutes).
- Sprinkle the chopped cilantro just before service.
- Serve with naan or paratha.

CHICKEN VINDALOO

SERVES: 4–6
PREPARATION: 4 hours marination; thereafter 20 minutes
COOKING: 30–35 minutes

"Vindaloo" is a term derived from the Portuguese word "Vinha De Alhos"—"Vinho" meaning wine or wine vinegar, and "Alhos" meaning garlic. After "Vinha De Alhos" was introduced in India it was re-created with spices and chillies.

INGREDIENTS

- 2 pounds boneless chicken—cut 1 inch
- 2 large Yukon potatoes—cut into 2 inch pieces
- 2 large onions—sliced long and thin
- 2 large tomatoes—diced
- 1 tablespoon cumin seeds
- 1 tablespoon cinnamon powder
- 3-4 red chillies—diced
- ½ tablespoon garlic-ginger paste
- 3 tablespoons white vinegar
- 2 tablespoons chili powder
- 1 tablespoon curry powder
- 4 curry leaves
- 1 cup quality cooking oil
- 1 cup water
- Salt to taste

METHOD

- Heat 2 tablespoons oil in a pan over medium heat. Carefully add cumin seeds, curry leaves, red chillies and fry for 30 seconds, stirring constantly. Let cool.

- Once cooled, take the pan fried spices, drain from the oil and blend in a blender with the cinnamon powder, garlic-ginger paste, chili powder, curry powder, salt, and 1 tablespoon vinegar into a paste. Be careful while blending.

- Take the spice paste and apply to the chicken pieces. Set aside for 3-4 hours.

- Heat the remaining cooking oil in a pot over medium-high heat and fry the potatoes until golden brown and just tender. Once the potatoes are fried, add the marinated chicken and diced tomatoes and cook on low heat.

- Add the remaining 2 tablespoons of vinegar and the 1 cup of water to the chicken and cook on a simmer. Cook until the chicken is "pull tender" and potatoes are cooked through.

- Finish with a sprinkle of cilantro.

EAST INDIAN CHICKEN CURRY

SERVES: 6 people
PREPARATION: 20–25 minutes
COOKING: 20–25 minutes

Mixed vegetables, chicken and boiled eggs in a red curry

INGREDIENTS

- 2 pounds skinless, boneless chicken—cut into 2 inch pieces
- 2 large tomatoes—diced
- ¾ cup red onion—diced
- 1 cup french green beans—diced
- 1 cup carrots—diced
- 1 cup green peas—diced
- 1 cup broccoli—diced
- 2 cage free eggs—boiled, peeled and sliced lengthwise
- 7 red chillies (Kashmiri dry chillies, can be found in any Indian grocery store). Soak them in warm water for 15 minutes
- 2 ½ cups coconut milk (canned is fine)
- ½ teaspoon garam masala
- ½ teaspoon cumin seeds
- 1 teaspoon cumin seeds
- 1 teaspoon coriander seeds
- 1 cinnamon stick
- ½ inch of fresh ginger root—diced
- 4 garlic cloves—diced
- 1 bunch cilantro—chopped
- ⅓ cup quality cooking oil
- Salt to taste

METHOD

- In a large pot, over medium-high heat, add the french beans, carrots, green peas, and broccoli and bring to a boil—add just enough water to cover the vegetables.

- Once the vegetables are tender and most of the water has evaporated, take it off the heat, remove any remaining water, and set aside.

- In a blender, add the chillies, cumin seeds, coriander seeds, onions, cinnamon stick, ginger and garlic. Add just enough water to process this mix to a thick paste.

- In a sauté pan, over medium-high heat, place this paste and cook for 5 minutes, stirring constantly so that it doesn't burn.

- After 5 minutes, add the chicken to the cooked paste and tomatoes. Cook for another 10 minutes.

- After 10 minutes, add salt to taste and the garam masala. Simmer until the gravy thickens and the chicken is cooked all the way through, stirring constantly.

- After the chicken is cooked, add the coconut milk and vegetables and bring to a quick boil. Cook for another 2-3 minutes. Stir constantly.

- After 2-3 minutes, transfer the contents of the pan to serving dish and add the cooked eggs and cilantro.

- Serve with Basmati rice.

GARLIC CHICKEN DRY

SERVES: 4–6
PREPARATION: 25 minutes
COOKING: 40 minutes

Boneless white meat chicken cooked with garlic-ginger paste and spices

INGREDIENTS

- 2 pounds skinless, boneless chicken breasts—cut into 2 inch pieces
- 2 large yellow onions— cut into 2 inch pieces
- 2 green bell peppers— cut into 2 inch pieces
- 1 bunch cilantro—chopped
- 2 cage free eggs—beaten
- 1 cup refined white flour
- 1 tablespoon chili powder
- 1 tablespoon garam masala
- 2 minced garlic
- ½ cup water
- 1 cup quality frying oil
- 2 tablespoons quality cooking oil
- 2 teaspoons salt

METHOD

- Mix together the beaten eggs, flour, salt and enough water to make a thick batter. Add the chicken and coat very well. Set aside for 5-10 minutes.

- Heat the oil in a deep frying pan on high heat, then carefully add each piece of chicken with the batter and fry to a golden brown. Keep the chicken pieces separated and circulating in the oil with a slotted metal spoon. After the chicken pieces turn golden brown all around, take them out with a straining spoon and place on paper towels. Set aside.

- In a sauté pan, heat 2 tablespoons of oil and stir fry minced garlic-ginger paste, onions and bell peppers until they are a bit shiny. This is a point where the onion and bell peppers have cooked a bit, but, are still crispy to the bite.

- Then add the fried chicken pieces with chili powder, garam masala and stir-fry for 5 minutes.

- Sprinkle with cilantro.

HONEY LEMON CHICKEN

SERVES: 4–6

PREPARATION: Overnight marination, or at least 1 hour, then 15 minutes remaining preparation.

COOKING: 40 minutes

A children's favorite at my restaurant Bombay Coast

INGREDIENTS

- 2 pounds skinless, boneless chicken breast
- ¼ cup fresh lemon juice
- ¼ cup yogurt
- ½ teaspoon cinnamon powder
- Tandoori masala—just a pinch to taste (available in Indian grocery store; or use recipe on pg. 26)
- ½ cup of honey
- 3 tablespoons sugar
- Salt to taste
- 2 tablespoons butter
- 6-8 inch bamboo skewers soaked in water for 30 minutes (12 pieces)

METHOD

- Cut chicken breast into 1 inch pieces and combine with lemon juice, yogurt, salt, cinnamon powder, tandoori masala and honey. Cover and put in the refrigerator for 1 hour.
- Thread 4-5 pieces of chicken onto skewers and spread remaining marinade on chicken.
- Apply butter on skewers and cook over barbeque grill.

KARAHI (WOK) CHICKEN

SERVES: 4–6
PREPARATION: 35 minutes
COOKING: 45–50 minutes

Boneless chicken cooked with stir fried bell peppers and onions

INGREDIENTS

- 2 pounds skinless, boneless chicken thigh—cut into 2 inch pieces
- 3 green bell peppers—cut into small squares
- 2 large yellow onions—cut into small squares
- 2 large tomatoes—chopped
- 1 bunch cilantro—chopped
- 2 green chillies—slit in half, remove seeds
- 4 teaspoons garlic-ginger paste
- 1 teaspoon ground coriander
- 1 teaspoon garam masala
- 3 tablespoons chopped ginger
- 1 tablespoon dry fenugreek leaves
- ½ cup quality cooking oil
- Salt to taste

METHOD

- Heat the oil in a wok or similar type of pan to medium-high heat, and add green bell peppers and onions, stir-fry for 5-7 minutes. Don't overcook as you want the pieces to have some bite to them. Take them out of the wok/pan and set aside in a bowl.

- In the same wok/pan, heat cooking oil to medium-high heat and add the garlic-ginger paste, ground coriander seeds and stir for a few seconds. Then add the tomatoes and bring to a boil.

- Once boiling, add half the cilantro leaves and all the ginger and salt and then lower to a simmer for 5 minutes.

- After 5 minutes, add the chicken and simmer, stirring occasionally until the gravy thickens and the chicken is tender.

- Once the fat surfaces, stir in the garam masala, dry fenugreek leaves, green bell peppers and onions and cook for another 2 minutes.

- Add cilantro and serve with Basmati rice.

MANGO CHICKEN MASALA

SERVES: 6
PREPARATION: 10 minutes
COOKING: 35–40 minutes

Chicken cooked in a mild creamy mango curry

INGREDIENTS

- 2 pounds skinless, boneless chicken—cut into 1 inch cubes
- 1 can of 30 ounce mango pulp
- 2 large yellow onions—diced
- 1 teaspoon turmeric powder
- 1 teaspoon coriander powder
- 2 cinnamon sticks
- 2 whole green cardamom pods
- 1 teaspoon cumin powder
- 1 cup whole organic milk
- 2 tablespoons heavy cream
- 1 tablespoon sugar
- ¼ cup water
- ¼ cup quality cooking oil
- Salt to taste

METHOD

- Heat cooking oil in a pan over medium high heat, add onions and fry until light brown, about 7-10 minutes.
- Add cinnamon sticks, green cardamom, turmeric powder, coriander powder, cumin powder to the onions, stirring occasionally.
- Add chicken and water; cook the chicken stirring occasionally for 10-12 minutes. Cook the chicken until it is golden brown.
- Add mango pulp, milk, sugar, stir well and cover for 10-15 minutes.
- Add cream and salt, stir well.
- Finish with a topping of diced mango pieces.

METHI MURGH

SERVES: 4
PREPARATION: 30 minutes marination; thereafter 15–20 minutes
COOKING: 35–40 minutes

Chicken cooked with fresh fenugreek (methi) leaves

INGREDIENTS

- 2 pounds skinless, boneless chicken—cut into 2 inch pieces
- 3 bunches of fresh fenugreek (Methi) leaves
- 2 large yellow onions—diced
- 2 large tomatoes—chopped
- 1 cup whole plain yogurt
- 1 bunch cilantro—chopped
- 3 tablespoons garlic-ginger paste
- 2 tablespoons ginger—slivered
- 5 pieces cardamoms
- 2 cinnamon sticks
- 5 pieces cloves
- 1 teaspoon chili powder
- 2 pieces green chillies—slit in half
- ½ cup quality cooking oil
- Salt to taste

METHOD

- Marinate chicken in yogurt and salt for half an hour.
- Over medium heat, quickly fry the cardamoms, cloves and cinnamon. After 1 minute, add onions and sauté until golden brown. Then add the garlic-ginger paste, slivered ginger, green chillies, chili powder and chopped tomatoes and cook on low-medium heat until the oil separates from the sauce.
- Add the marinated chicken and 1 cup water, bring to boil, cover and simmer until the fat is visible on the sides once again and the chicken is tender.
- Add fresh fenugreek leaves (methi), stir and simmer for 5 minutes.
- Add cilantro and serve with roti.

MURGH (CHICKEN) MUSALLAM

SERVES: 4–6
PREPARATION: 20 minutes
COOKING: 40 minutes

Sweet and sour chicken with a hint of clove and cardamom.

"Murgh" means chicken, and "Murgh Musallam" means whole chicken. Murgh Musallam is a Mughlai dish that was popular amongst the royal families of the Mughal rule in India.

INGREDIENTS

- 6 pieces of skinless, boneless breasts of chicken or drum sticks
- 4 large yellow onions—sliced
- 12 pieces whole red chillies
- ½ tablespoon clove powder
- 8 pieces green cardamom
- ½ tablespoon whole cloves
- 2 tablespoons garlic-ginger paste—diluted in 2 tablespoons water
- 1 tablespoon fresh lemon juice
- 1 tablespoon fresh lemon juice
- ¼ cup water
- ½ cup quality cooking oil
- Salt to taste

METHOD

- Heat the oil in a wok over medium-high heat, fry ⅔ of the onions until golden brown along with the whole red chillies. Remove, cool and puree the onion-red chili mix.
- Fry the remaining onions in the same oil and add the diluted garlic-ginger paste. Add the whole cloves and green cardamom, stir well, and cook for another 2-3 minutes.
- Add the chicken and fry for another 5 minutes on high heat.
- Add the clove powder and salt, cook until well browned.
- Add the pureed onion-chili puree and brown for another 10-15 minutes until the oil rises to the surface.
- Finally, add the lemon juice and honey to make it sweet and sour.

RESHMI KEBAB (SILKEN KEBAB)

SERVES: 6–10

PREPARATION: Overnight marination; 20 minutes thereafter

COOKING: 30–50 minutes

A traditional Mughlai dish. The meat becomes so tender and juicy, almost silky to the tongue, because of the time it marinates.

INGREDIENTS

- 2 pounds skinless, boneless chicken breast—cubed
- 6 almonds
- 6 cashew nuts
- 3 green chillies
- 2 teaspoons garlic-ginger paste
- ½ cup heavy cream
- ⅓ cup fresh lemon juice
- 1 cup cilantro—chopped
- Salt to taste
- 6 bamboo skewers, soaked in water overnight

METHOD

- Place almonds in a small bowl and cover with warm water. Allow to soak for 15 to 30 minutes. After soaking, remove the skins from the almonds.

- Place almonds, cashew nuts, green chillies, garlic-ginger paste, and cilantro into a food processor, blend until smooth, season with salt.

- Place chicken in a bowl, add the heavy cream, lemon juice and nut mixture, stir, cover and put in refrigerator and marinate overnight. If you can't marinate overnight, at least marinate for 2 hours.

- Thread 4 to 5 pieces of chicken onto skewers and put remaining marinade onto chicken.

- Roast chicken skewers over barbeque grill until the chicken is cooked (juices run clear), use a good extra virgin olive oil to lightly coat chicken on the skewers prior to cooking.

- Serve with tamarind chutney.

SAFFRON (RED GOLD) CHICKEN

SERVES: 4–6

PREPARATION: 1 hour marination of chicken (includes 20 minutes soaking of other ingredients; thereafter 20 minutes)

COOKING: 35–40 minutes

Chicken in a rich saffron curry

INGREDIENTS

- 2 pounds skinless, boneless chicken—cut in 1 inch cubes
- 2 large yellow onions—sliced, fried and then blended to a puree
- ¼ cup whole plain yogurt
- 1 bunch cilantro—chopped
- 2 tablespoons garlic-ginger paste
- ½ teaspoon chili powder
- ⅓ cup cashew nuts
- A few strands of saffron
- 2 bay leaves
- 2 green cardamoms
- 1 teaspoon garam masala
- 1 cup whole organic almond milk
- 2 tablespoons heavy cream
- ¼ cup water
- ⅓ cup quality cooking oil
- Salt to taste

* It is important to soak the strands of saffron in warm almond milk overnight, otherwise the real taste of saffron and its beautifully vibrant red/yellow color will not seep into your dish. Use the almond milk that the saffron has soaked in as well as the strands. Dried saffron can store in a cool, dry and dark place for up to two years.

METHOD

- Place the cubes of chicken in a mixing bowl and add yogurt, garlic-ginger paste, salt and chili powder. Mix well and leave to marinate for at least 1 hour. Cover the bowl.

- Soak the cashew nuts in ¼ cup water and set aside for 20 minutes. Then grind the cashews into a smooth paste. Set the paste aside.

- Meanwhile, heat 2 tablespoons of oil in a sauté pan over medium-high heat and sauté the sliced onions until light golden brown. Then remove the onions, let cool and then puree in a blender.

- Heat the remaining cooking oil in a pan on medium-high heat. Once hot, carefully add the bay leaves, cardamom, onion puree and cook until the mixture is light to golden brown. Stir constantly as the mixture will burn easily due to the temperature and natural sugars in the onions.

- After the mixture is light to golden brown, bring the temperature up to high heat and add the marinated chicken. Then cook the chicken for another 5 minutes, stirring constantly so that the chicken doesn't burn on one side.

- After 5 minutes, reduce the heat to medium and add the cashew paste and cook until the liquid evaporates and the oil separates. Stir constantly.

- Add the milk and ¼ cup water, cover and cook until the chicken is tender.

- Add the saffron strings and its almond milk to the mixture, stir well.

- Garnish with cilantro and serve.

TANDOORI CHICKEN

SERVES: 4
PREPARATION: Overnight marination, or at least 2 hours; thereafter 15 minutes
COOKING: 30 minutes

Tandoori chicken originated in the Punjab region of India. It is the way the chicken is cooked that makes it unique—in a clay earthen oven at high temperatures. It's quick to cook and the marinade does all the work.

INGREDIENTS

- 2 pounds boneless, skinless chicken breast—cut into 1 inch pieces
- 1 cup whole plain yogurt
- 4 teaspoons tandoori masala (available in Indian grocery store; or use recipe on pg. 26)
- 1 teaspoon salt
- 2 teaspoons quality extra virgin olive oil
- Cilantro for garnish

METHOD

- In a medium bowl, combine salt, yogurt, tandoori masala and chicken and mix well. Cover the bowl and leave to marinate in the refrigerator overnight or for at least 2 hours.
- Heat a grill to medium-high heat, lightly oil the surface and roast the marinated chicken over the grill. Grill the chicken until the juices run clear.

FISH & SHRIMP

(Machhalee and Jheenga)

CHEESE FISH FILLETS
WITH HOT TOMATO SAUCE

DUM JHINGA ANARI

FISH CAKES

FISH IN COCONUT MILK

GRILLED KING PRAWNS
WITH STIR-FRIED SPICES

JHINGA (SMALL SHRIMP)
MALAI CURRY

MADRAS FISH CURRY

MALABAR SHRIMP CURRY

SHRIMP KEBAB

TANDOORI FISH

A Visit to the Fish Market in Bombay

Bombay's historical trade and occupation is evidenced by the various countries and international companies that laid claim to her shores. The shores of Bombay can tell very intriguing and fantastic true stories.

One of those fantastic and empire building stories involves the existing Sassoon Dock. This dock was established by David Sassoon & Co., Ltd. David Sassoon was a Baghdadi Jewish businessman who immigrated with his family to Bombay from Baghdad.

Mr. Sassoon got his start acting as a middleman between British textile firms and Gulf commodity merchants. Thereafter he endeavored in purchasing his shoreline properties in Bombay.

Sassoon competed mainly with Parsis in the opium and textile trade with China. David Sassoon became very prosperous and soon ventured in the oil and mill businesses. Many synagogues, hospitals, schools and The Gateway of India were built by David Sassoon and his company's wealth.

The Docks, which were built by Sassoon's son Albert Abdullah David Sassoon, were the first commercial wet docks in Bombay. The Docks were built on reclaimed land in South Bombay.

Visiting Sassoon Dock is not a trip to the fish market, it's a trip to another world that resembles the 1800s in Bombay. Not much has changed as far as buying fish, especially the smell, but, the amount of buyers and sellers has and the type of goods sold.

When I ran the Ideal Corner restaurant located in Fort Bombay, I used to go to the Sassoon Docks by 6:30 am and buy fish and shrimp sold at auction. It was a real experience and a nasty one at that. You got hit in the ribs, pushed and shoved around in order to buy up the best catches from the various vendors.

When I went to the docks, I wore gum boots and an old shirt because there's fish water everywhere. The fisherwomen sit opposite each other on raised wooden platforms and shout and scream to attract the attention of clients.

It was a great benefit to become a regular buyer, because the fisherwoman would reduce her price just for you. It became a standard game for the fisherwoman to state a high price for the fish. We had to bid her down by slashing her price to less than 50% of what she had quoted and then bid her lower until she settled for a decent price.

I used to buy Pomfret fish. It is one of the most popular fish in Mumbai. One can find this type of fish in the Asian food stores in the U.S. There is a recipe in this section for this fish.

In this section of my cookbook, there are many delicious and easy recipes for fish and shrimp that you can make and experience what I have growing up in Bombay. And more importantly, you can experience the history of the fish market, Sassoon Dock, in your home.

CHEESE FISH FILLETS
WITH HOT TOMATO SAUCE

SERVES: 6
COOKING TIME: 30 minutes marination; thereafter 10 minutes
PREPARATION: 30 minutes

INGREDIENTS

- 3 pieces white meat fish fillets—skinned
- 1 large yellow onion—sliced
- 1 pound tomatoes—skinned, deseeded and pureed
- 1 beetroot—boiled and sliced
- 1 lemon—sliced
- A few leaves of butter lettuce
- 4 cage free eggs—beaten
- 2 cups quality grated cheese (your preference)
- 2 cucumbers—sliced
- 2 bunches parsley—chopped
- 1 teaspoon corn flour
- 2 cups toasted bread crumbs
- 2 teaspoons fresh lime juice
- 2 teaspoons black pepper powder
- 1 tablespoon freshly chopped mint
- 4 cups quality frying oil
- Salt to taste

HOT TOMATO SAUCE:

- 1 cup tomato ketchup
- 1 tablespoon tabasco sauce
- 1 teaspoon sugar
- 1 teaspoon Worchester sauce
- 1 tablespoon corn flour

METHOD

- Wash the fish fillets and marinate in salt, lime juice and black pepper powder. Let the fillets sit for 30 minutes.

- Whisk eggs with the corn flour in a shallow bowl.

- Heat the 4 cups of oil over medium-high heat in a large frying pan.

- Coat one side of the fish with the grated cheese. Then on the other side of the fish, dip it in the egg mixture and then coat that side with the bread crumbs. Deep fry each fillet until golden brown on both sides. Start with the breaded side and then turn gently onto the cheese side.

- Tie 3 sprigs of parsley in a bunch and deep fry.

- Arrange the fish fillets on a flat dish on top of the lettuce, onion slices, cucumber, beetroot and lemon wedges.

- Place the fresh tomato puree in a sauce pan along with the ketchup, tabasco, sugar, Worchester sauce and corn flour. Stir over a high flame and bring to a fast boil. Once it starts to boil. Immediately remove from the heat, add salt to taste.

- Serve the tomato sauce along with fillets.

DUM JHINGA ANARI

SERVES: 4
COOKING TIME: 30 minutes marination; thereafter 10 minutes
PREPARATION: 20 minutes

Large prawns cooked with pomegranate seeds and spices

INGREDIENTS

- 20 large prawns or jumbo shrimp—peeled, deveined
- 1 large pickled onion—sliced (available in Indian grocery store)
- 2 tablespoons cheddar cheese —shredded
- ½ cup whole plain yogurt
- ½ cup green peas (fresh/frozen)
- 1 cup pomegranate seeds
- 3 tablespoons tomato ketchup
- 1 teaspoon garlic-ginger paste
- ½ teaspoon white pepper powder
- ½ teaspoon red chili powder
- 1 tablespoon cilantro —finely chopped
- ½ tablespoon cumin seeds
- 2 tablespoons fresh lemon juice
- 2 tablespoons malt vinegar
- Salt to taste

METHOD

- Mix the malt vinegar, salt, red chili powder, garlic-ginger paste and shrimp in a bowl. Let it marinate for 30 minutes.
- Boil, drain and mash the peas.
- Then in a bowl, mix the mashed peas with the yogurt, shredded cheese, onion, cilantro, cumin seeds, lemon juice, white pepper, ketchup and pomegranate seeds.
- Place each shrimp on a separate 10 inch square piece of greased aluminum foil.
- Top each shrimp with the mashed pea mixture.
- Place the shrimp on the foil on a baking tray and bake in a preheated oven of 325 degrees Fahrenheit for 15 minutes.
- Serve with fresh chappati.

FISH CAKES

SERVES: 4–5
COOKING TIME: 25 minutes
PREPARATION: 15 minutes

These tasty fish cakes can be made slightly larger and served as a fish burger, or formed into small balls to serve as cocktail snacks.

INGREDIENTS

- 2 large pieces of white fish—skinned
- 2 medium potatoes—boiled and mashed
- 4 green onions—diced
- 2 green chillies—diced
- 1 piece fresh ginger root—diced
- 1 bunch of cilantro—chopped
- 2-6 mint leaves—finely chopped
- 1 teaspoon ground black pepper
- 2 cage free eggs
- Bread crumbs
- 2 cups quality cooking oil
- Salt to taste

METHOD

- Place the fish in a lightly greased steamer and steam until cooked. Once cooked, remove the pot from the heat or turn off the steamer and set aside.

- Place the potatoes, green onions, green chillies, ginger, cilantro, mint, black pepper and 1 egg in a large bowl. Mix well. When the fish is cool, crumble coarsely into the bowl and mix well. Shape the mixture into cakes.

- Beat the remaining egg in a separate shallow dish and dip the cakes in it then coat lightly with the bread crumbs.

- Heat the cooking oil in a frying pan over medium-high heat and fry the cakes until brown on all sides. Once lightly browned (do not overcook as the fish is already cooked from the steaming), remove and place the fish cakes on a paper towel to remove any excess oil.

- Serve with sweet tamarind chutney or spicy chutney.
  (available in Indian grocery store; or use recipes on pg. 233 and 230)

FISH IN COCONUT MILK

SERVES: 4–5

PREPARATION: 15 minutes marination; thereafter 15 minutes

COOKING: 25–35 minutes

It is a delicate flavored curry, easy to make. It is served with Basmati rice

INGREDIENTS

- 6 large pieces white meat fish—skinned
- 1 large yellow onion—chopped
- 4 green chillies—slit in half
- 1 can pureed tomato
- 6-8 curry leaves
- 3 tablespoons garlic-ginger paste
- ¼ teaspoon turmeric powder
- ¼ teaspoon fresh lime juice
- 1 can coconut milk
- 3 tablespoons quality cooking oil
- Salt to taste

METHOD

- Marinate the fish by mixing half of the turmeric powder, lime juice and salt. Rub this mix all over the fish pieces and leave for 15 minutes.

- Heat the cooking oil in a broad-based cooking pot on medium-high heat, then sauté the onions, chillies, and garlic-ginger paste until the onions are golden. This will take about 10 minutes. Then add the tomato puree and curry leaves.

- After 2 minutes add the coconut milk and remaining turmeric and cook for 10 minutes over a low heat. Stir occasionally.

- After 10 minutes, add the fish pieces and stir very lightly otherwise the fish will break apart. Cook until the fish is done.

- Serve with Basmati rice.

GRILLED KING PRAWN

WITH STIR-FRIED SPICES

SERVES: 4

PREPARATION: 30 minutes marination; thereafter 15 minutes

COOKING: 40 minutes

Traditionally king prawns are marinated and then grilled in the tandoor oven or a very hot electric or gas grill as in this recipe.

INGREDIENTS

- 16-20 peeled, deveined king prawns (jumbo shrimp)
- 3 large yellow onions—sliced
- 1 yellow bell pepper—diced
- 1 red bell pepper—diced
- 1 tablespoon cilantro—finely chopped
- 3 tablespoons whole plain yogurt
- 1 teaspoon garlic-ginger paste
- 1 teaspoon fresh ginger root—grated
- 1 teaspoon paprika powder
- ½ teaspoon fennel seeds—crushed
- 1 cinnamon stick
- 1 teaspoon chili powder
- 1 tablespoon quality cooking oil
- Salt to taste

METHOD

- In a large bowl, place the shrimp, yogurt, paprika powder, garlic-ginger paste and salt. Lightly mix. Let the mixture sit for 30 minutes.

- Meanwhile, heat the oil in a wok or large pan over medium-high heat and fry the sliced onions with the fennel seeds and the cinnamon stick. Once the onions are light golden, lower the heat and stir in the garlic-ginger paste, chili powder, yellow and red bell peppers and stir fry gently for 5 minutes.

- Preheat a grill to medium-high heat and place the marinated shrimp (prawns) on the grill to darken their tops and get a good char on the surface. Once the shrimp are lightly charred, add them to the onion and spice mixture and garnish with fresh cilantro.

- Serve with Basmati rice and creamy black lentils.

JHINGA (SMALL SHRIMP) MALAI CURRY

SERVES: 4
PREPARATION: 15 minutes marination
COOKING: 30–40 minutes

Creamy mild tomato shrimp curry

INGREDIENTS

- 20 pieces small shrimp—peeled and deveined
- 4 tablespoons tomato puree
- ½ cup heavy cream
- 3 tablespoons fresh lemon juice
- ½ teaspoon granulated sugar
- 1 small green chili—minced
- ½ teaspoon cumin powder
- ½ teaspoon cardamom powder
- ½ teaspoon chili powder
- 1 teaspoon garam masala
- 3 tablespoons garlic-ginger paste
- ½ teaspoon mustard seeds
- 10 curry leaves
- 1 bunch cilantro—chopped
- 3 tablespoons quality cooking oil
- Salt to taste

METHOD

- Put the cream, tomato puree, sugar, lemon juice, green chili, ground cumin powder, cardamom powder, chili powder, garam masala and some salt in a bowl. Mix together and set aside.

- Heat the cooking oil in a shallow frying pan over high heat, when hot, carefully add the mustard seeds, when the seeds begin to pop, add the curry leaves. Then lower the heat to medium, add the garlic-ginger paste and fry for 30 seconds, stirring constantly.

- After 30 seconds, add shrimp and fry for 2-3 minutes on each side, being careful not to overcook them as this can make them hard and rubbery.

- Pour the entire cream-tomato-spice mixture from the bowl into the pan, stir well, cover and simmer on low heat for 3 minutes.

- Finish with a sprinkling of cilantro.

- Serve with Basmati rice.

MADRAS FISH CURRY

SERVES: 5–6
PREPARATION: 30 minutes for soaking and marination; thereafter 15 minutes
COOKING: 15 minutes

A fish gravy that is pungent and thick

INGREDIENTS

- 4 large pieces of fish—skinned
- 2 large tomatoes—chopped
- 2 large yellow onions—chopped
- 3 slices fresh ginger root—diced
- 6 garlic cloves
- 20 curry leaves
- 6 teaspoons poppy seeds—crushed
- 1 ½ teaspoons tamarind pulp
- ¼ teaspoon mustard seeds
- ¾ teaspoon fenugreek seeds
- 3 tablespoons coconut powder
- 1 teaspoon coriander powder
- ½ teaspoon turmeric powder
- 2 teaspoons chili powder
- 1 teaspoon paprika powder
- ¾ teaspoon cumin powder
- 1 teaspoon fresh lime juice
- 2 teaspoons apple cider vinegar
- ½ cup quality cooking oil
- Salt to taste

METHOD

- Soak the tamarind in water for 30 minutes, strain and set aside.

- Marinate the fish in the lime juice, vinegar, and a little salt for 30 minutes.

- In a blender, put the coconut powder, ginger, garlic-ginger paste, tomatoes and poppy seeds. Do not add any water, process for 30 seconds.

- Heat the cooking oil in a shallow cooking pot over medium-high heat. Add the mustard seeds. As soon as they start popping, add the onions and fry until they turn golden brown. Then, add the curry leaves, coriander, turmeric and chili powders and stir fry for 3 minutes.

- After 3 minutes, add the coconut mixture and sauté for 5 minutes, stirring constantly. Then add the tamarind water, salt and a cup of water, bring to a boil and then reduce to a simmer and cook for 3 minutes. After 3 minutes, gently add the fish pieces in a single layer and keep the heat to low, cook for an additional 1-2 minutes until fish is just done.

- Sprinkle with mixture of fenugreek and cumin seed.

MALABAR SHRIMP CURRY

SERVES: 6–10
PREPARATION:
1 hour soak for tamarind;
20 minutes food preparation
COOKING: 45 minutes

This is a famous curry recipe they cook in the Malabar region of Kerala. They cook shrimp in a terracotta pot and use coconut oil, but that has a particular taste. We will cook it in coconut milk.

INGREDIENTS

- 16 to 20 shrimp—peeled, deveined and uncooked
- 2 large tomatoes—chopped
- 1 large yellow onion—sliced
- 1 tablespoon tamarind pulp (see below to make; also available ready-made in Indian grocery store)
- 1 can coconut milk
- 3 tablespoons garlic-ginger paste
- ¼ teaspoon mustard seeds
- 16 curry leaves
- 4 green chillies—cut in half
- 2 dried red chillies—broken into pieces
- 1 teaspoon red chili powder
- ½ teaspoon turmeric powder
- ½ teaspoon coriander powder
- ½ teaspoon cumin powder
- 2 cups water
- 3 tablespoons quality cooking oil
- 2 tablespoons Indian ghee
- Salt to taste

METHOD

- Soak the tamarind seeds in warm water for about an hour. After an hour, take each seed and squeeze them to get the remaining pulp into the water. Mix the pulpy mixture very well, and set aside.
- Add the cooking oil to a pan and heat to medium-high. Then add the mustard seeds. When they start to pop, add the curry leaves, and after a few seconds add the sliced onions and sauté, stirring for 10 minutes. Thereafter, add the garlic-ginger paste and green chillies. Stir well for 5 minutes.
- After the 5 minutes add the dried red chili, chili powder, turmeric powder, coriander powder and cumin powder. Stir well. Then add 2 tablespoons of water and cook for 8-10 minutes, constantly stirring so that nothing sticks to the bottom of the pan.
- Add the chopped tomatoes, 1 cup water and the tamarind pulp. Turn the heat down and let it simmer for 8-10 minutes. Then, after the 8-10 minutes, add the coconut milk and salt and cook for an additional 3 minutes, stirring occasionally.

- After the 3 minutes, add the shrimp and cook over a low heat until the shrimp turn a bright pink. Be careful as shrimp cook quickly.

- To add a delightful finishing touch to the curry just before service, take a deep ladle and place 2 tablespoons of a fine extra virgin olive oil or Indian ghee in the ladle. Then hold the ladle over high heat. When the oil is hot, add the remaining curry leaves and flash fry them. Once done, top the curry with the extra virgin olive oil and curry leaves. If you want, you can use more curry leaves for this part of the recipe.

- Serve with a fresh garnish of chopped cilantro.

SHRIMP KEBAB

SERVES: 6–10
PREPARATION: 20 minutes
COOKING: 35 minutes

Shrimp marinated with herbs and spices served with deep fried potatoes

INGREDIENTS

- 20 pieces king prawns (jumbo shrimp)
- 1 large yellow onion—diced
- 2 cage free eggs—beaten
- 2 large potatoes—boiled
- 1 tablespoon cumin seeds
- 10 black peppercorns
- 6 green chillies—deseeded and minced
- 1 teaspoon poppy seeds
- 2 tablespoons garlic-ginger paste
- 1 cup fresh lemon juice
- 1 bunch cilantro—finely chopped
- ½ cup bread crumbs
- 1 cup quality cooking/frying oil
- Salt to taste

METHOD

- Grind the following without using any water, and then after grinding the spices, mix by hand the boiled potatoes, mashing them while you mix:
  - Cumin seeds
  - Garlic-ginger paste
  - Green chillies
  - Peppercorns
  - Poppy seeds
  - Boiled potatoes
- Dice the shrimp. Then to the grinded mix, add the prawns/shrimp, salt to taste and mix well.
- Add the onion with the beaten eggs, lemon juice and chopped cilantro.
- Fold the onion-egg mix in with the shrimp mixture.
- Then, wet your hands and start rolling the shrimp mixture into balls—any size to your liking.
- In a frying pan, heat the cooking/frying oil to medium-high. Take the balls and coat each with bread crumbs and deep fry in the hot oil.
- Take care not to fry too many at one time as this will cook the oil and the balls will soak up the oil instead of frying quickly.
- Once they turn golden brown, take them out and place them on a paper towel to soak up any excess oil.
- Serve hot with mango or peach and mint chutneys.
- Peach chutney recipe on pg. 238.

TANDOORI FISH

SERVES: 4–5
PREPARATION: 20 minutes marination; thereafter 20 minutes
COOKING: 25–35 minutes

Fish baked in a tandoor oven with herbs and spices or baked on a grill

INGREDIENTS

- 7 pieces Salmon or Mahi-Mahi fish—cubed, skinned
- 3 tablespoons cilantro—chopped
- 3 teaspoons fresh lemon juice
- 1 cup of whole organic yogurt
- ¼ teaspoon turmeric powder
- 1 teaspoon coriander powder
- ¼ teaspoon garam masala
- 1 teaspoon paprika powder
- 1 tablespoon melted butter for basting
- Salt to taste

METHOD

- In a flat dish, drizzle the fish with the lemon juice and some salt, turmeric powder and coat both sides. Set aside for about 5-7 minutes.
- In a shallow dish, add yogurt, coriander powder, garam masala, paprika powder and a little salt. Mix well.
- Add the fish to the yogurt mixture and thoroughly coat fish. Turn each piece to make sure the fish is evenly coated. Cover and set aside to marinate for at least 20 minutes.
- Preheat a grill to high. Cover the grill with greased foil and place the fish on this, and grill for 5 minutes on each side or until golden brown. Baste with melted butter half way through the cooking time before turning over. The middle of the fish should turn from almost a jelly opaque white or pink to a firm white or pink (depending on what fish you use).
- Serve with onions and lime wedges.

VEGETARIAN

(Shaakaahaaree)

PANEER

ALOO GOBI

ALOO JEERA

BAINGAN BHARTA

CHANNA MASALA

DAL AND SPINACH

KOFTA CURRY

KADHAI PANEER

NAVRATTAN KORMA

PALAK (SAAG) PANEER

PANEER MAKHANI

PANEER TAWA MASALA (PANEER BHURJI)

PUNJABI DAL (BLACK DAL)

Being a vegetarian is not a requirement to enjoying vegetarian dishes. And one would think that vegetarian dishes are bland, boring and so tremendously healthy as to make one sick of being that healthy.

In fact the opposite is true for Indian vegetarian dishes. Vegetarianism originated from India and Greece. In India, the idea was to preserve a non-violent attitude towards animals called "ahimsa". Ahimsa is Sanskrit for "compassion" and refers to non-violence. In ancient Greece, the practice of vegetarianism was called "abstinence from beings with a soul".

Vegetarianism goes further in India than just the "meat", orthodox Hindus and Jains do not use garlic or onions in their cooking and do not have raw onions in their salads. In addition, the middle class families in North and Central India view that meat eating is for the men and not the women, as the meat induces a violent nature that is more natural for a man.

Vegetarian dishes are so varied and tasty that one would not know that they are eating a purely vegetable dish until told. The use of spices, cooking techniques and a plentiful list of vegetables allows so many selections that anyone will able to find something they like. Vegetables like artichoke, winter melon, bananas, beetroot, bitter gourd, fava beans, cucumber, cabbage, eggplant, fenugreek, french green beans and cilantro are some of the most recognized.

However, unique vegetables that are used in Indian cooking include ivy gourd, jack fruit, lady fingers (okra), lotus root, green mango, mango ginger, tapioca, tamarind, water chestnuts, amaranth leaves, coconut, curry leaves, snake gourd, taro roots, elephant yam, mint leaves, balloon vine, bamboo shoot, betel leaf, and radish pods—just to name a few.

With this variety, most of my recipes in this section will not only satisfy, but, also exceed the most of conservative palates. To begin, the recipes offered here are some of the most popular in India and here in the West. At my restaurant in San Diego, these recipes are my customers' favorites.

Part of the vegetarian diet that helps make the vegetarian palate so diversified, delicious and nutritious is the combination of vegetables with various legume seeds called pulses. Legumes are a significant source of protein, dietary fiber, carbohydrates and minerals. The term "dal" refers to a split pulse, but, not hulled. One will find pulses in various forms of dishes throughout India as this grain seed is a universal source of a nutrient rich food. India is the worlds' largest producer and consumer of pulses.

The most common varieties of split pulses are the Toor dal (yellow pigeon peas) often found in Sambar, Chana dal (black chickpeas), yellow split peas (one of the most popular forms of dal), Mung/moong dal (split mung beans), Urad dal (black gram) found in idli and dosa dishes, Masoor dal (split red lentils) and Panchratna dal (five varieties of dal).

PANEER

PREPARATION: 7–10 minutes
COOKING: 20 minutes
Set aside for 2 hours

This traditional North Indian cheese is made from rich dairy milk. Paneer is white in color and has a smooth texture. Paneer is very easy to make at home and doesn't require aging or culturing. Because paneer won't melt or get gooey in hot dishes, paneer can take the place of a non-vegetarian item in a dish to make it vegetarian.

INGREDIENTS

- 4 cups whole organic milk
- 2 tablespoons fresh lemon juice
- 1 cheese cloth
- Pinch of salt

METHOD

- Bring 4 cups of milk to a boil over a medium heat, then as soon as it starts to boil lower the heat to a simmer. Keep stirring so that the milk doesn't scald at the bottom of the pot. When the milk looks foamy remove it from the heat and stir in the lemon juice.

- Stir gently until the milk thickens and begins to curdle. Let the curdled milk sit for 10 minutes. Thereafter, the liquid should look yellow and watery.

- Strain the curdled milk through a sieve lined with the cheese cloth.

- Pull the sides of the cheese cloth up together and then twist the ball of curdled milk until you squeeze as much liquid out as possible. You are separating the curds from the whey at this point.

- Tie the cheese cloth with the curds in it, like a sack and place a heavy weight on top so that the curds form into a flat slab about ½ inches thick and the remaining liquids drain. Set aside for 2 hours.

- Thereafter, cut into wedges and use as required. Paneer will keep for up to 1 week in the refrigerator.

ALOO GOBI

SERVES: 4–6
PREPARATION: 25 minutes
COOKING: 40 minutes

Potatoes (aloo) and cauliflower (gobi) cooked with herbs and spices

INGREDIENTS

- 2 cauliflowers—broken into florets
- 3 large potatoes—diced
- 1 large yellow onion—diced, fried and pureed
- 1 large tomato—chopped
- 1 teaspoon garlic-ginger paste
- ½ teaspoon garam masala
- 1 teaspoon chili powder
- 1 tablespoon coriander powder
- 1 teaspoon cumin powder
- 1 teaspoon mustard seeds
- 1 tablespoon turmeric powder
- 3 cups water
- 4 tablespoons quality cooking oil
- Salt to taste

METHOD

- Scrub the potatoes and cut them into small pieces. Boil the potatoes and cauliflower in water with salt and turmeric powder for 10-15 minutes or until al dente. Drain the potatoes and cauliflower and set aside.

- In the meantime, heat a sauté pan to medium-high and fry the diced onion until just golden brown, about 8 minutes. Once done, remove from heat, let cool and puree in a blender. Set aside.

- In another pan, heat to medium heat and add the tomatoes and sauté until the tomatoes become soft, approximately 5 minutes. Once the tomatoes are done, set aside in a side bowl.

- In the same pan, heat 2 tablespoons of oil to medium-high. Then add the garam masala, chili powder, garlic-ginger paste, coriander powder, cumin powder and mustard seeds and simmer for about 5 minutes, stirring constantly.

- After 5 minutes, add the potatoes and cauliflower and stir for another 5 minutes. Thereafter, add the pureed onions, tomatoes, and 1 cup of water stirring well to ensure everything is evenly mixed. First bring to a boil, then once it starts to boil, reduce the heat, cover and cook until the cauliflower is tender but still has a bite to it. Cook longer if you prefer softer cauliflower. Mix well.

- Serve hot with naan.

ALOO JEERA

SERVES: 6
PREPARATION: 10 minutes
COOKING: 25 minutes

Potatoes cooked with cumin seeds and spices

INGREDIENTS

- 3 large potatoes—cubed and boiled
- 2 large yellow onions—chopped
- 1 green bell pepper—diced
- 1 cup cilantro—chopped
- 1 tablespoon turmeric powder
- 6-8 curry leaves
- 2 tablespoons cumin seeds
- 1 green chili—minced
- 2 tablespoons red chili powder
- 1 tablespoon fresh lemon juice
- 3 tablespoons quality cooking oil
- Salt to taste

METHOD

- Peel the potatoes under cold running water and cut them into small pieces. Boil the potatoes in water with little salt and ½ teaspoon of turmeric powder for 10-15 minutes or until tender. Drain the potatoes and set aside.

- Heat oil in a frying pan over medium-high and add the cumin seeds and let them sizzle for about 20 seconds. Then, add the onions and bell peppers. Cook until the onions are soft and just golden brown.

- Once the onions are soft, add the potatoes, curry leaves, cumin seeds, green chillies, red chili powder, salt and a tablespoon of water. Cook over a low heat for about 10 minutes stirring well to ensure the spices are evenly mixed.

- Add cilantro and lemon juice to taste and serve with paratha.

BAINGAN BHARTA

SERVES: 4
PREPARATION: 20 minutes
COOKING: 25 minutes

This eggplant dish is prepared with exotic herbs and spices

INGREDIENTS

- 4 large eggplants (aubergine/baingan)
- 1 large onion—chopped
- 1 large tomato—diced
- 1 bunch cilantro—chopped
- 1 teaspoon garlic-ginger paste
- 1 teaspoon cumin seeds
- 1 tablespoon red chili powder
- 1 teaspoon turmeric powder
- 1 teaspoon coriander seeds
- 10 curry leaves
- ½ cup mustard oil
- Salt to taste

METHOD

- Wash the eggplants thoroughly and pat dry. Then roast all four whole eggplants on a griddle or in an oven for 10-15 minutes. After they are soft, remove from oven and mash them in a bowl. Set aside.

- Heat the mustard oil in a broad based cooking pot over medium-high. Then add the onions and fry until golden brown. Once brown, add the diced tomatoes, garlic-ginger paste, cumin seeds, curry leaves, turmeric powder, and red chili powder and stir well. Add a little water if the spices begin to burn. Cook for 8-10 minutes, constantly stirring.

- Thereafter, add the eggplant and 2 cups of water to the pot. Simmer for 10 minutes or until the water has evaporated, but the mix should not be completely dry. It should be a moist mixture but not watery either.

- Sprinkle cilantro just before serving.

- Serve with roti.

CHANNA MASALA

SERVES: 6
PREPARATION: Overnight for soaking; 20 minutes actual preparation
COOKING: 40 minutes

Chickpeas (garbanzo beans) cooked in a medium spicy curry. They are made in a black spice mix with a dominant flavor of cumin.

INGREDIENTS

- 1 pound fresh garbanzo beans or 1 can chickpeas (or garbanzo beans)
- 3 large yellow onions—chopped
- 4 tomatoes—skinned, chopped and deseeded (can buy canned)
- 2 tablespoons garlic-ginger paste
- 8 garlic cloves—minced
- 2 tablespoons cumin powder
- 1 teaspoon turmeric powder
- 1 teaspoon garam masala
- 1 teaspoon coriander powder
- 1 cinnamon stick
- 2 tablespoons fresh lemon juice
- 5 cups of water
- ½ cup cilantro—chopped
- 3 tablespoons quality cooking oil
- Salt to taste

METHOD

- Soak the chickpeas in 4 cups of water overnight. After they have been soaking overnight, rinse them under running water. Or if you are using garbanzo beans from a can then drain the garbanzo beans and rinse them under running water. With either the soaked beans or the canned beans, while rinsing them under the water take the skins off, drain and set aside.

- Puree the tomatoes separately in a food processor and set aside.

- Heat the cooking oil to medium-high in a pot and add the onions and fry them until golden brown. Once brown add the garlic-ginger paste, minced garlic, cumin and sauté for 5 minutes.

- Once brown, add the tomato puree, turmeric powder, garam masala, coriander powder, and cinnamon stick and mix well for 1 minute.

- Then, add the garbanzo beans and 2 cups of water and stir thoroughly. Cook until the garbanzo beans are tender, add salt to taste.

- Right before service, add the chopped cilantro and lemon juice and incorporate them well.

- Serve with Bhatura (thick leavened fried Indian bread) or Pooris (unleavened deep-fried Indian bread).

DAL AND SPINACH

SERVES: 6
PREPARATION: 15 minutes
COOKING: 65 minutes

Yellow split lentil (Dal) cooked with fresh spinach (Palak), herbs and spices

INGREDIENTS

- 1 pound yellow split lentil (dal)
- 2 bunches fresh spinach—chopped
- 2 large yellow onions—diced
- 4 large tomatoes—diced
- 4 green chillies
- 2 ½ tablespoons turmeric powder
- ½ tablespoon chili powder
- 1 tablespoon cumin seeds
- 4 tablespoons quality cooking oil
- 6 cups of water
- Salt to taste

METHOD

- Wash and strain the raw dal twice in lukewarm water to remove any foreign matter or small stones that occur in the handling of the harvesting of the dal and then set aside.

- Heat 2 tablespoons of cooking oil in a frying pan to medium-high. Then, add the onions, tomatoes, and chillies and sauté for 10 minutes or until the onions turn golden brown and then set aside.

- Heat the remaining 2 tablespoons of cooking oil in another pot/pan to medium-high and add the clean raw dal along with 6 cups of water and bring to a boil. Boil for 30 minutes until the dal becomes mushy. Alternatively, you can place the dal in a pressure cooker. This is a preferred way as it takes less time and is much easier to determine when the dal is done correctly.

- When the dal is cooked, rough mash it, like home style mashed potatoes. Rough mash it in the same cooking pot, reduce the heat to medium-low.

- Then, after the dal is rough mashed, add the turmeric powder, chili powder, cumin seeds and stir those in well. Stir well and let that sit for 10 minutes.

- After 10 minutes, in the same pot as the mashed dal, add the cooked onions, tomatoes and chillies mix along with the freshly chopped spinach leaves. Cook this for another 10 minutes. Add salt to taste.

- Serve hot with Basmati rice.

KADHAI PANEER

SERVES: 4
PREPARATION: 15 minutes
COOKING: 25-30 minutes

This hot curry with paneer is an all-time favorite

INGREDIENTS

- 2 pounds paneer—cubed into 2 inch pieces
  (available in Indian grocery store; or use recipe on pg. 132)
- 1 large green bell pepper—cubed into 2 inch pieces
- 1 large yellow onion—cubed into 2 inch pieces
- 2 large tomatoes—chopped
- 3 teaspoons cilantro—chopped
- 1 teaspoon garlic-ginger paste
- 2 tablespoons fresh ginger root—chopped
- 10-12 dry red chillies
- 4 green chillies—chopped
- 3 teaspoons coriander seeds
- 1 teaspoon garam masala
- 1 teaspoon dry fenugreek leaves (kasoon methi)
- ½ cup quality cooking oil
- Salt to taste

METHOD

- Pound the red chillies and coriander seeds into a powder; you can use a grinder as well, but, be careful of the red chillies and wait a few seconds before uncovering after grinding. There might be powder that sprays in the air.
- In a broad based cooking pot heat 5 tablespoons oil over medium-high heat. Add the garlic-ginger paste and sauté quickly until very light brown. To the same pot, add ½ of the ground red chillies and coriander seed powder from above, the diced green chillies and ginger, and sauté for 30 seconds to 1 minute.
- Then to the same pot, add the tomatoes, stir and cook until the fat surfaces. Thereafter, add the dry fenugreek leaves, salt and garam masala. Stir well, put the heat on low and set aside.
- In another pan, heat the remaining oil on medium-high. Add the bell peppers and onions, and sauté for 30-45 seconds.
- To the onion and bell pepper pan, add the remaining ½ of the pounded coriander and dry red chili powder, stir well, reduce the heat to low and cook until the oil surfaces/separates from the main liquid. After the separation of the oil and the liquid, add the paneer and stir gently for 5 minutes. After 5 minutes, add the onion and bell pepper contents to the pot with the tomato contents. Stir well to incorporate all the ingredients.
- Sprinkle the cilantro over the top just before service.
- Serve with Basmati rice.

KOFTA CURRY

SERVES: 4
PREPARATION: 40 minutes
COOKING: 1 hour

Vegetables dumplings in rich gravy

INGREDIENTS

FOR KOFTAS

- 1 cup gram flour (garbanzo bean flour)(besan)
- 1 pound paneer—crumbled
- 1 large yellow onion—diced, fried and pureed
- 1 Yukon gold potato—boiled and mashed
- 1 bunch of cilantro—chopped
- ½ cup carrots—diced
- ½ cup green beans—diced
- ½ cup green peas
- 2 green chillies—minced
- 1 tablespoon broken cashew nut pieces
- 1 tablespoon garlic-ginger paste
- 1 tablespoon cumin powder
- 5 tablespoons quality frying oil

FOR GRAVY

- 2 tablespoons cashew nut paste (available in natural grocery stores)
- 1 large yellow onion—chopped
- 1 bunch of cilantro—chopped
- ½ cup tomato puree
- 1 tomato—chopped
- 1 tablespoon coriander powder
- ½ teaspoon garam masala
- 1 tablespoon heavy cream
- 1 tablespoon garlic-ginger paste
- ½ teaspoon turmeric powder
- ½ tablespoon cumin seeds
- 2 tablespoons quality cooking oil
- Salt to taste

METHOD

KOFTAS

- Take a big bowl and add paneer, broken cashew nuts, cilantro, carrots, green beans, green peas, onions, garlic-ginger paste, mashed potato, and cumin powder and mix well. Then add the gram flour and a little water. Mix all ingredients for the koftas.

- Divide the mixture into golf ball size portions. Form the balls by rolling each portion between the palm of your hands.

- In a deep pot for frying, heat the 5 tablespoons of frying oil on medium-high heat deep fry the balls until golden brown. You want to make sure that the gram flour is cooked through or else it will be raw. Once golden brown, keep aside on paper towels.

GRAVY

- In a frying pan, heat 2 tablespoons of the cooking oil over medium heat. Add the chopped onions and fry until they turn golden brown and become translucent. Then add the garlic-ginger paste, cashew nut paste, garam masala, turmeric and salt. Fry for 3 minutes. After 3 minutes, add the chopped tomato and tomato puree and cook for another 10 minutes, stirring constantly. Then, add ½ cup of water and simmer on low heat until the gravy starts to thicken.

- Once the gravy starts to thicken, add the heavy cream and the fried koftas to the gravy. Stir gently, but, thoroughly incorporating all ingredients.

- Garnish with cilantro and serve while hot.

NAVRATTAN KORMA

SERVES: 6
PREPARATION: 15 minutes
COOKING: 20 minutes

A mixed vegetable delight with the goodness of 9 types of vegetables

INGREDIENTS

- 2 large yellow onions—diced
- 2 large tomatoes—diced
- 12 cashew nuts
- ½ teaspoon garlic-ginger paste
- ½ cup french green beans—diced
- ½ cup carrots—diced
- 3 ounces broccoli—separate so you have the little florets
- 3 ounces cauliflower—separate so you have the little florets
- 3 ounces green peas
- 3 ounces potatoes—diced
- 3 ounces zucchini—cut
- 3 ounces mushrooms (any preference)
- 1 ounce sweet corn
- 2 bay leaves
- 3 pieces cardamoms
- 5 tablespoons coconut powder
- 2 teaspoons turmeric powder
- Salt to taste

METHOD

- Blend the coconut, cashew nuts, onions, garlic-ginger paste, turmeric powder and tomatoes in a blender.
- In a pot, on medium-high heat, boil all the vegetables. Put just enough water to cover the vegetables because we want to boil the water away and leave the contents with the spices in it. Add the bay leaves, cardamoms, salt, and cook for about 10 minutes.
- Once the vegetables are tender and the water has evaporated add the blended paste and stir well. Cook for 5-10 minutes.
- Serve with roti.

PALAK (SAAG) PANEER

SERVES: 4
PREPARATION: 20 minutes
COOKING: 40 minutes

Fresh spinach and paneer cooked in herbs and spices

INGREDIENTS

- 2 pounds paneer—cut 1 inch cubes (available in Indian grocery store; or use recipe on pg. 132)
- 2 bundles of fresh spinach—chopped
- 2 large yellow onions—chopped
- 2 large tomatoes—chopped
- 3 tablespoons heavy cream
- 1 tablespoon garlic-ginger paste
- 1 green chili—minced
- 2 tablespoons dry fenugreek leaves (kasoon methi)
- 1 teaspoon cumin seeds
- 1 tablespoon chili powder
- 2 teaspoons coriander powder
- ½ teaspoon garam masala
- 2 tablespoons quality cooking oil
- Salt to taste

METHOD

- Wash spinach leaves and blend them with ½ cup of water into a puree.

- Heat the cooking oil in a broad based cooking pan to medium-high. Then add the cumin seeds, garlic-ginger paste, onions, green chillies, coriander powder and garam masala. Sauté for 5 minutes in order to cook the spices. Be careful when cooking spices dry as they release oils and the aroma can be very pungent to the nose, throat and eyes.

- Thereafter, add the chopped tomatoes, the (kasoon methi) dry fenugreek leaves, the spinach puree, and the chili powder to the pan, mix well, and cook for another 5 minutes. Stir constantly.

- After 5 minutes, add the heavy cream, salt to taste and paneer. Stir gently so that you don't break up the paneer pieces. Simmer for 5 minutes.

- After the 5 minutes, serve with hot paratha.

PANEER MAKHANI

SERVES: 4
PREPARATION:
10 minutes for soaking;
30 minutes overall preparation
COOKING: 45 minutes

Paneer cook in a mild buttery cream curry

INGREDIENTS

- 1 pound paneer—cubed
  (available in Indian grocery story;
  or use recipe on pg. 132)
- 2 tablespoons butter or ghee
- 5 large tomatoes—chopped
- 1 piece of fresh
  ginger root—minced
- 4 tablespoons cashew nuts
  (soaked in ¼ cup of water
  and ground to a paste)
- 1 tablespoon ketchup
- 4 crushed green cardamoms
- ½ teaspoon sugar
- ½ teaspoon garam masala
- ½ teaspoon chili powder
- 2 teaspoons dry fenugreek leaves
- 1 cup whole organic milk
- 4 tablespoons heavy cream
- 2 tablespoons quality cooking oil
- Salt to taste

METHOD

- Soak the cashew nuts in warm water for 10 minutes. After 10 minutes, grind them to a paste. Set aside.

- Puree tomatoes and ginger and set aside.

- Heat the cooking oil over medium-high in a broad based cooking pot. Add the cardamoms, sugar, garam masala, chili powder and mix all the ingredients. Cook for 3 minutes.

- Then add the tomato-ginger puree and ketchup. Mix well and cook for another 8-10 minutes.

- After 10 minutes, add the cashew nut paste, dry fenugreek leaves and ½ cup of water, stir well and cook for another 5 minutes.

- Thereafter, add the paneer and the milk to get thick red gravy. Boil for 5 minutes. After boiling for 5 minutes add butter, cream and salt and continue to boil for another 5 minutes, stirring constantly. Thereafter, turn down the heat and simmer for another 5 minutes.

- Serve hot with Basmati rice.

PANEER TAWA MASALA (PANEER BHURJI)

SERVES: 4
PREPARATION: 15–20 minutes
COOKING: 30 minutes

This is a unique preparation of paneer cooked on a griddle

INGREDIENTS

- 1 pound paneer—cubed (available in Indian grocery store; or use recipe on pg. 132)
- 1 large onion—chopped
- 2 large tomatoes—chopped
- 1 green bell pepper—cubed
- 1 bunch of cilantro—chopped
- 2 tablespoons garlic-ginger paste
- ½ teaspoon black cumin seeds
- 1 teaspoon coriander powder
- 1 teaspoon cumin powder
- ½ teaspoon garam masala
- 1 teaspoon chili powder
- 1 green chili—chopped
- 3 tablespoons quality cooking oil
- Salt to taste

METHOD

- Heat the griddle pan to medium-high and add 3 tablespoons of oil. When the oil is hot, add the black cumin seeds and onions. Cook the seeds and onions until light brown, approximately 10 minutes. Stir frequently.

- After 10 minutes, add the garlic-ginger paste, cumin powder, garam masala, chili powder, green chillies and green bell peppers. Cook on medium heat for 10 minutes.

- After 10 minutes, add the chopped tomatoes and cook until the oil separates from the gravy and rises to the surface.

- Once the oil separates, add paneer, salt and cilantro. Stir the paneer into the gravy/sauce gently so as not to break up the pieces of paneer. Cook approximately 5-7 minutes on low heat.

- Serve hot with fresh chappati.

PUNJABI DAL (BLACK DAL)

SERVES: 6
PREPARATION: Overnight soaking or at least 3 hours; thereafter 25 minutes
COOKING: 1 ½ hours

Black lentils and black eye peas cooked with herbs and spices

INGREDIENTS

- 10 ¾ ounces whole black lentils
- 10 ¾ ounces black eyed peas
- 1 tablespoon chili powder
- 2 tablespoons dal makhani powder (available in Indian/Asian stores)
- 2 tablespoons garlic-ginger paste
- ½ cup of tomato puree
- 2 tablespoons quality cooking oil
- 6 cups of water
- Salt to taste

METHOD

- Clean and strain the dal, then soak the dal for at least 3 hours (my Mom used to soak it overnight).

- In a big pot over low heat, add the dal and 6 cups of water. Simmer until the dal splits and becomes soft enough to mash. Once done, mash the dal in the pot.

- Then, add the tomato puree, garlic-ginger paste, salt, dal makhani powder, chili powder and cook for 60 minutes or until the dal and liquid become thick.

- Add 2 tablespoons of oil and cook for another 15 minutes, stirring continuously until the fat is incorporated into the dal.

- Serve with brown rice and fried pappadum.

RICE DISHES

(Chaaval)

BOILED BASMATI RICE

CHICKEN BIRYANI

GREEN PEAS & MUSHROOM RICE

HERB, SHRIMP & FISH PULAO RICE

LAMB PULAO

SOUTH INDIAN LEMON RICE

Delivering bags of rice in Bombay

BOILED BASMATI RICE

SERVES: 5
PREPARATION: 30 minutes soaking; thereafter 35 minutes
COOKING: 35–45 minutes

INGREDIENTS

- 1 pound Basmati rice
- 9 ½ ounces of water
- ½ teaspoon of quality cooking oil
- Salt to taste

METHOD

- It is best to cook the rice about 1 hour before the service of the meal.

- In a bowl, add cold water just enough to cover the rice. Swirl the rice around the bowl with your hand. This will cause the starch to leech into the water and that helps the rice to stay separate when you cook it. Carefully, drain the starchy water and repeat this rinse. Thereafter, soak the rice in fresh lukewarm water for 30 minutes. The rice will expand 25% during this time.

- After 30 minutes, rinse the rice and add the 9 ½ ounces of water into the pot and place the pot on the stove. Heat the water to a boil, add salt and the oil. When the water starts to boil, add the rice, stir and let the rice boil for 10 minutes. The rice will cook to about 95% done. Once 10 minutes is over, reduce the heat as low as possible and cover the pot. Cook for another 5 minutes and then uncover to release the excess moisture. Stir gently with a fork to air and dry the rice.

CHICKEN BIRYANI

SERVES: 8-10
PREPARATION: 30 minutes
COOKING: 60 minutes

Biryani is a meal in itself and needs no accompaniment, except for a yogurt raita.

INGREDIENTS

- 4 skinless, boneless chicken breasts—cubed into 1 inch pieces
- 1 ¼ cup ghee (clarified butter)
- 2 ½ cups Basmati rice-washed and then soaked (uncooked) in water for 1 hour
- ½ cup of whole organic yogurt
- 1 pinch of saffron threads—soaked in 4 tablespoons hot whole organic milk
- 6 teaspoons red chili powder
- 4 teaspoons ginger—minced
- 3 tablespoons coriander powder
- ¾ teaspoon cumin powder
- ½ teaspoon clove powder
- 4 bay leaves
- ½ cup of water
- 5 teaspoons salt
- Dutch Oven or similar deep, heavy bottomed pot for final cooking of the biryani
- Fresh lime, chopped cilantro and sliced red onion for garnish

METHOD

- In a cup, soak the saffron threads in the 4 tablespoons of hot/warm milk. Set aside.

- In a deep pot, over medium heat, heat 1 cup of the ghee and add the chicken pieces, the yogurt, salt, red chili powder, scrapped ginger and ½ cup of water. Stir well while the water evaporates.

- Once the water has evaporated, add the coriander powder, cumin powder, clove powder and saffron included the milk it has been soaking in. Stir everything very well and let it cook for 10 minutes. Simmer on low heat until the water dries up completely and only the ghee remains.

- In a separate pot, boil the rice (please see Boiled Basmati Rice recipe on pg. 163). When just cooked, drain the rice completely. On a flat baking pan, divide the cooked rice into four parts.

- In the deep, heavy bottomed pot (like a Dutch Oven), heat ¼ cup of ghee on medium heat and make sure the bottom and sides have a coating of that same ghee so that rice will not stick for the final cooking.

- Take one part of the four parts of rice and spread it on the bottom of the pot, then spread ½ of the cooked chicken mixture over the rice. Cover that with two more parts of the rice and two bay leaves. Then spread the remaining chicken mixture over that along with one bay leaf. Finally, spread the remaining one part of rice over the chicken mixture and add the final bay leaf on top of that. Cover the pot and cook it over low heat to form steam inside the pot to cook the rice all the way through, approximately 10-15 minutes. As soon as the steam starts to rise, open the lid and stir the contents lightly.

- Garnish with cilantro, red onion and lime and serve.

GREEN PEAS AND MUSHROOM RICE

SERVES: 6
PREPARATION: 30 minutes
COOKING: 60 minutes

INGREDIENTS

- 2 ½ cups Basmati rice
- 1 large tomato—sliced
- 2 cups button mushrooms
- 1 cup sweet green peas (frozen or fresh)
- 1 teaspoon cumin seeds
- 2 cardamom pods
- 2 cinnamon sticks
- 3 garlic cloves—sliced
- 4-5 cups of water
- 2 tablespoons quality cooking oil
- Salt to taste

METHOD

- Wash the uncooked rice twice, drain and set aside in a strainer (See Boiled Basmati Rice recipe on pg. 163).

- In a medium sauce pan, heat the oil over medium-high and add the cumin seeds, cardamom, cinnamon sticks, sliced garlic, sliced tomato, button mushrooms and salt. Stir fry for 5 minutes.

- After 5 minutes, add the rice and peas and gently stir around, making sure you do not break the rice.

- Add the water and bring the mixture to a boil. Once it starts to boil, reduce the heat to low and cover. Continue to cook for 15-20 minutes. As soon as steam rises, open the lid and stir lightly.

HERB, SHRIMP AND FISH PULAO RICE

SERVES: 6
PREPARATION: 35 minutes
COOKING: 35 minutes

Medium spicy rice is cooked with shrimp and fish

INGREDIENTS

- 2 cups raw Basmati rice
- 12 pieces large shrimp—shelled, deveined and washed
- 6 pieces white fish fillets
- 2 large tomatoes—skinned and pureed
- 4 green onions—julienned
- 1 garlic clove—sliced
- 2 green bell peppers—julienned
- 2 tablespoons fresh thyme—chopped
- 2 tablespoons parsley—chopped
- 2 celery stalks—diced
- ½ cup of cilantro—chopped
- 2 star anise
- 2 bay leaves
- 2 tablespoons unsalted butter
- 1 tablespoon sugar
- Salt to taste

METHOD

- Wash the rice twice and cook in a rice cooker with star anise, bay leaves, salt and butter (or use the Basmati Rice recipe on pg. 163).
- Wash the shrimp and fish fillets. Sprinkle salt all over the shrimp and fish fillets and set aside.
- In a blender, add the tomatoes, sugar and a pinch of salt. Puree the mix. Set aside.
- In a wok or frying pan over medium-high heat, add the butter and fry the green onions, garlic, green bell peppers, thyme, parsley and celery. Cook for 5 minutes, stirring continuously.
- After 5 minutes, add the tomato puree and bring to a boil. Once at a boil add the fish filets and reduce the heat to medium and cook for 8-10 minutes.
- After 8-10 minutes, add the shrimp and cook until the shrimp turns an opaque white, no longer as you do not want the shrimp to get tough. Then, once the shrimp is done, place the rice in a big flat dish and arrange the shrimp and fish in layers.
- If any fish or shrimp are left over place on top of the rice.
- Garnish with cilantro.

LAMB PULAO

SERVES: 6
PREPARATION: 30 minutes
COOKING: 90 minutes

A pulao is a deep, rich tasting rice dish containing whole spices with meat. My Mom used to make this dish for special occasions. She would serve it with the Dhansakh Dal (traditional Parsi Dal).

INGREDIENTS

- 3 cups raw Basmati rice
- 1 pound lamb—cubed
- 2 large yellow onions—sliced
- 2 large tomatoes—sliced
- 2 tablespoons whole organic yogurt
- 4 tablespoons cilantro—chopped
- 1 teaspoon garlic-ginger paste
- ½ teaspoon chili powder
- ½ teaspoon turmeric powder
- 1 teaspoon garam masala
- 4 green cardamom pods
- 4 cloves
- ½ teaspoon cumin seeds
- ½ teaspoon saffron strands—soaked in 2 tablespoons of hot whole organic milk
- 1 tablespoon fresh lime juice
- 4 tablespoons quality cooking oil
- 5 cups water
- Salt to taste

METHOD

- Wash the uncooked rice twice, drain and set aside.

- In a deep pot, heat 4 tablespoons cooking oil over medium-high, add the onions and fry until golden brown and translucent.

- Lower the heat to medium and add the garlic-ginger paste, chili powder, garam masala, turmeric powder, salt, yogurt and tomatoes and stir fry gently for 5 minutes.

- After 5 minutes, add the lamb and turn up the heat to high. Use a slotted spoon to fry the lamb, scraping the bottom of the pan to prevent it from burning. Add the cilantro and continue to stir well. Once the lamb is thoroughly cooked, set the pot to one side.

- Put the raw rice into a large sauce pan with the water, cloves, cardamom, cumin seeds and salt and bring to a boil. (See Boiled Basmati Rice recipe on pg. 163). When the rice has cooked, drain the water. Remove half of the rice from the boiling pot. Take the lamb mixture and place that on the bottom portion of the rice in the boiling pot. Then take the removed rice and place it back over the lamb mixture in the boiling pot. Add the saffron with the milk and lime juice all over the rice-lamb mixture, cover the pot and cook on very low heat for 20 minutes.

- After 20 minutes, carefully remove the lid, and garnish with cilantro.

- Serve hot with dal.

SOUTH INDIAN LEMON RICE

SERVES: 5
PREPARATION: 10 minutes
COOKING: 40–50 minutes

Yellow rice flavored with mustard seeds and lemon, ground turmeric is used to give color and white dal adds crunch to the rice.

INGREDIENTS

- 1 cup raw Basmati rice
- 5 cups water
- 3 tablespoons fresh lemon juice
- ½ tablespoon mustard seeds
- 2 tablespoons white urad dal
- 3 dry red chillies—broken into pieces
- 5 curry leaves
- 5 tablespoons quality cooking oil
- Salt to taste

* Urad dal is a "white lentil" that is actually the interior of the whole urad bean, also known as the black gram. Urad dal is used to make Idli-Dosa, Vada, Papad/Pappadum and is highly nutritious.

METHOD

- Wash the uncooked rice and then boil it (see Boiled Basmati Rice recipe on pg. 163).

- In a small bowl, whisk the lemon juice, turmeric, salt and sugar together and set aside.

- Heat 2 tablespoons cooking oil in a large wok to medium-high, reduce the heat to medium and then add mustard seeds, white urad dal and dry red chillies. Once you add them stir quickly for 30 seconds and then reduce the heat to low and cook until the urad dal turns light brown. Once the urad dal turns light brown add the curry leaves and stir well.

- Then, add the lemon juice mixture, ¼ cup of water and cover. Simmer on low heat until the urad dal becomes soft and the water evaporates. Once the water has evaporated, fork through the rice to separate the rice grains. Stir gently to mix well.

- Serve hot with yogurt.

INDIAN BREADS

(Rotee)

BHATURA/POORIS

NAAN

PLAIN PARATHA

STUFFED PARATHA

WHOLE WHEAT CHAPPATI

Indian dishes are often served with breads. You will find that naan, chappati and the deliciously flaky paratha are surprisingly easy to make at home. The indigenous breads of India are unleavened breads known as roti made from ground whole wheat flour.

Traditionally, naan is baked in a tandoor clay pot oven. However, you can bake them in the conventional oven and the naan looks and tastes just as authentic. Increasingly, one can find ready-made naan at the local specialty stores, such as Trader Joe's, or Sprouts.

However, when making the chappati, you will need to have a griddle because placing the chappati in the oven will dry it out.

BHATURA/POORIS

SERVES: 5 pieces
PREPARATION: 3–4 hours dough proofing; thereafter 15 minutes
COOKING: 20 minutes

Bhaturas are deep fried puffed bread made with unleavened dough. The semolina makes it crisp. You can serve with channa masala, aloo (potato) or dal and spinach.

INGREDIENTS

- 2 cups of Maida* flour (in the U.S., cake flour can be used as a substitute)
    * Maida flour is finely milled refined and bleached wheat flour, like cake flour, or plain/all-purpose flour from India. It is used for bread, cakes, chappatis, parathas and pooris.

- 2 teaspoons yeast
- ½ cup luke-warm water
- ½ cup semolina (Suji)
- ½ teaspoon salt
- 2 tablespoons whole organic yogurt
- 1 teaspoon granulated sugar
- Quality frying oil for deep frying

METHOD

- Mix the yeast with the sugar and water in a bowl. Set aside.

- In another bowl, sift the flour and then stir in the semolina (Suji) and salt.

- Add the yeast mixture and yogurt to the flour mixture and mix the dough. Turn out the dough on to a lightly floured surface and knead for 10 minutes until smooth and elastic. Roll the dough into a big ball and lightly brush the dough with oil. Keep covered in a warm place for 3-4 hours.

- After 3-4 hours, turn the dough out on to a lightly floured surface and divide the dough into ten equal pieces and shape each into a ball. Flatten into a round with the palm of your hand. Roll each ball out on a lightly floured surface into 5 inch rounds.

- In a deep frying pan, heat the frying oil to medium-high. Once hot, carefully slide 1 bhatura or poori into the oil. Fry for about 1 minute turning over after 30 seconds. Remove from oil before they turn brown. Then drain well on kitchen paper towel.

- Serve hot. Pooris go well with channa masala and raita.

NAAN

SERVES: 10 pieces
PREPARATION: 2 hours dough proofing; thereafter 30 minutes
COOKING: 8–10 minutes

Traditionally naan is made with all-purpose flour and is hot rolled, patted and stretched until the teardrop shape is achieved.

INGREDIENTS

- 2 cups all-purpose flour (plus extra for dusting)
- 1 tablespoon sugar
- 1 teaspoon dried yeast
- ⅔ cups warm water
- 1 teaspoon ghee (clarified butter)/unsalted butter
- Salt to taste

METHOD

- Put the sugar and yeast into a small bowl and add warm water. Mix to dissolve the yeast. Set aside for about 10 minutes.

- Sift the flour in a large bowl, make a well in the middle and add the ghee, salt and yeast mixture. Mix well using your hands, and adding a little more water if the dough is too dry.

- Turn the dough out on to a lightly flowered surface and knead for about 5 minutes, or until formed into a doughy ball. If you have a mixer, feel free to use it instead of kneading the dough by hand.

- Return the dough to the bowl, cover and leave in a warm place for about 2 hours, until it has doubled in size.

- After 2 hours, break off small pieces of the dough with your hand, and roll into rounds about 13 cm. in diameter and ½ inch thick. Roll out each ball to an oblong shape.

- **COOKING:** A tandoor oven is used to cook the naan. The tandoor oven is very large and used in restaurants. So, the alternate method is grilling the naan on a griddle or grill. Lightly oil the grill/griddle and place the formed naan on it. Cook for about 2-3 minutes or until puffy and lightly browned. Brush the uncooked side with butter or ghee and turn over. Cook the same. Keep turning the naan over until it is cooked completely. When done, brush one side of the naan with butter or ghee as preferred. You can also sprinkle minced garlic and cilantro for garlic naan.

PLAIN PARATHA

SERVES: 6 parathas
PREPARATION: 30 minutes for dough proofing; thereafter 15 minutes
COOKING: 15 minutes

A pan fried flat bread. Paratha is very popular Indian breakfast bread. The plain parathas are served with yogurt raita.

INGREDIENTS

- 1 cup whole wheat flour
- 2 teaspoons quality cooking oil (ghee can be substituted)
- ¾ cup water
- Salt to taste

METHOD

- In a mixing bowl, sift the salt and whole wheat flour.
- Add water to the dry mix to form dough. Then, add 1 teaspoon cooking oil to the dough and knead well until smooth. Cover and set aside for at least 30 minutes.
- After 30 minutes, take the dough and divide into 6 smooth equal sized balls.
- Dust a rolling surface with some flour, take a ball and flatten it slightly in your hands, then roll it out into a medium circle—about 5 inches in diameter.
- Heat a medium-sized griddle to medium-high heat and drizzle a few drops of cooking oil on the surface. The griddle should not get too hot as it will burn the outside of the paratha and leave the inside raw.
- Carefully place the paratha on the griddle and cook each side approximately 2-3 minutes. Continue the same process for the remaining parathas.
- Serve hot with yogurt raita and your favorite Indian dish.

STUFFED PARATHAS

SERVES: 4
PREPARATION: 20 minutes
COOKING: 10 minutes

These are pan fried flat breads which are stuffed with spicy potatoes, green peas, and carrots.

INGREDIENTS

- 2 Yukon gold potatoes—cooked and coarsely mashed
- 2 cups whole wheat flour
- ¾ cups of water
- 1 cup green peas
- 1 large carrot—diced
- ½ teaspoon garam masala
- ½ teaspoon red chili powder
- ½ teaspoon turmeric powder
- 2 tablespoons cilantro—chopped
- 2 tablespoons oil/unsalted butter
- Salt to taste

METHOD

- Mixed salt and whole wheat flour in a bowl. Add water to get dough of rolling consistency. Knead well until smooth. Cover and set aside for at least 30 minutes.
- **FILLING**: Boil the potatoes and mash them. In a bowl, add the mashed potatoes, garam masala, red chili, turmeric, cilantro, green peas and carrots. Mix well until all ingredients are thoroughly combined. Set aside for 15 minutes so that the ingredients can blend together.
- Take two balls of dough and roll them out into very thin rounds. Then take a spoonful size of filling and dollop it into the middle of the round. Cover that round with the other round. Press the edges together to form a tight seal. Do the same for the remaining rounds and filling. You can use an egg wash or plain water to seal the edges.
- On medium heat, place a griddle or large pan and add a few drops of cooking oil. Don't let the griddle/pan get too hot or you will burn the paratha before it can cook all the way through. Carefully pick up the paratha and put it on the griddle/in the pan. When the underside is cooked (approximately 2-3 minutes) turn to cook the other side. Trickle some butter on top. Cook for 2-3 minutes. Continue the same process with the remaining parathas.
- Serve hot and with plain yogurt or raita.

WHOLE WHEAT CHAPPATIS

SERVES: 10
PREPARATION: 12 minutes
COOKING: 20 minutes

Chappatis are prepared daily in most Indian homes. They are made with whole wheat flour.

INGREDIENTS

- 3 cups whole wheat flour (extra for dusting)
- 3 tablespoons water
- 1 teaspoon salt
- ½ teaspoon quality cooking oil
- 1 tablespoon unsalted butter or ghee

METHOD

- Sift the flour and salt into a large bowl. Make a well in the center and slowly add small quantities of water, until you have pliable dough. Grease the palms of your hands and knead the dough well. Once properly formed, keep the dough covered until you are ready to use.
- Divide the dough into 10-12 equal portions. Using 1 portion at a time and keeping the rest covered, knead each portion into a ball. Flatten the ball with your hands and place on a floured surface. Roll out until you have a circle about 7 inches in diameter.
- Heat a heavy griddle on high and brush lightly with cooking oil. When the griddle gets hot, roast the chappatis on each side pressing the edges down gently as the dough will form hot air pockets throughout the dough as it cooks. When both sides are ready brush the first side lightly with butter or ghee.
- Serve hot.

PARSI DISHES

CHICKEN LIVER GRAVY
WITH GIZZARDS

DHANSAKH DAL

FISH TAMATAR

FRIED BROWN RICE

EGG BHURJI

EGG CURRY

GREEN CHICKEN CURRY

KERA-PER-EDA
(EGGS AND FRIED BANANAS)

KHEEMA CURRY

KOLMI-NO-PATIO

LAMB JARDALOO SALLI BOTI

MARGHI-NA-FARCHA

MUTTON KEBAB

PARSI PORO

PATRA-NI-MACHI

TARELI MACHI

P arsi dishes are almost always complimented with a side salad called Kachumber Salad. It is a refreshing side salad made with diced tomato, cucumber, onion, radish, cilantro, lemon juice and salt.

CHICKEN LIVER GRAVY WITH GIZZARDS

SERVES: 6–8

PREPARATION: 10 minutes for spices to marinate; thereafter 25 minutes

COOKING: 25–30 minutes

INGREDIENTS

- 2 pounds chicken liver
- 1 pound gizzards
- 2 large Yukon potatoes—peeled and cubed
- 2 large yellow onions—sliced
- 2 large tomatoes—diced
- 6 pieces whole red chillies
- 1 jaggery piece—crushed
- 2 tablespoons garam masala
- 1 tablespoon garlic-ginger paste
- 1 tablespoon chili powder
- 2 tablespoons white vinegar
- 3 cups water
- ½ cup quality cooking oil
- Salt to taste

(jaggery is a course dark brown sugar made from evaporated palm tree sap—
it tastes like brown sugar and caramel. You can buy this from any Indian food store)

METHOD

- In a bowl, combine the jaggery, whole red chillies, garam masala, and chili powder in the vinegar and set aside. Let this sit for 10 minutes.
- Clean the livers and cut each into two pieces, wash and set aside.
- Clean and skin the gizzards, wash and cut them into small pieces. Use a pressure cooker to cook the gizzards by adding two cups of water and cook until soft. Drain the gizzards.
- Heat a pan to medium-high and quickly fry the potatoes in 2 tablespoons of cooking oil. Once the potatoes are light golden brown, remove from the heat and set aside.
- In another pan, heat cooking oil on medium-high, add the blended spices prepared in the vinegar above and cook for 5 minutes, stirring constantly as the spices will tend to burn if left in sitting in the pan. Watch your eyes and your nose, as vapors from the cooking spices tend to irritate them. Add the boiled gizzards and 1 cup of water to the spice pan and allow to simmer for 10 minutes. During the cooking, shake the pan from side to side so that the gizzards do not stick to the pan. After 10 minutes remove the pan from the heat.
- In a medium pan, heat 2 tablespoons of oil, add the onions and tomatoes and sauté over medium to medium-low heat for 15 minutes, stirring occasionally, until tender. Once tender, add the gizzards, liver, potatoes, blended spice-vinegar mixture and cook on medium heat for 8-10 minutes.
- After 8-10 minutes, remove from heat and serve with a garnish of fresh cilantro.

DHANSAKH DAL

SERVES: 6–8
PREPARATION: 20 minutes for soaking; thereafter 25 minutes
COOKING: 90 minutes

Pink lentils cooked with special dhansakh masala and vegetables

INGREDIENTS

- 1 pound pink masur/masoor dal
  (pink masur/masoor dal is processed from black masur lentils—the skin is removed and the grains are split—pink masur dal can be found at any Indian grocery store or online)

- 1 small red pumpkin—cubed
- 1 small eggplant—cubed
- 2 large tomatoes—chopped
- 1 bunch green onions—diced
- 2 ½ tablespoons cilantro—chopped
- 3 green chillies—deseeded and minced
- 1 small bunch of fenugreek fresh leaves
- 5 curry leaves
- 1 tablespoon turmeric powder
- 1 tablespoon chili powder
- 2 tablespoons parsi dhansakh masala (available in Indian grocery store)
- 1 ½ tablespoon garlic-ginger paste
- 1 cup ghee or unsalted butter
- 6 cups water
- Salt to taste

METHOD

- Wash the dal twice (put in a pot with water, swirl it around with your hand to remove any debris that occurs naturally in the harvesting and packaging process; do this twice). Once washed, soak the dal in water for 20 minutes.

- While the dal soaks, wash and chop the green onions, red pumpkin, eggplant, and fenugreek leaves.

- After 20 minutes of soaking, drain the dal and place into a round deep pot with 2 tablespoons of ghee/butter.

- Add the green onions, red pumpkin, eggplant and fenugreek leaves to the lentils, along with the turmeric powder, chili powder, garlic-ginger paste and salt. Add 6 cups of water and cook until the dal becomes soft.

- When the Dal is done take it out and puree in a blender. Be careful as the dal is still hot and it has a tendency to pop up while blending. Blend on low and slowly increase. If you need, blend in batches. If the dal is too thick, add a bit of water to thin as preferred. Once pureed, set aside.

- In a small frying pan add 2 tablespoons ghee, the chopped tomatoes, curry leaves, dhansakh masala and stir for 5 minutes.

- Add the pureed dal in pot and add fried masala sauce from above. Simmer for 15 minutes, stirring occasionally.

- Once cooked, serve the dhansakh with lamb biryani or over plain Basmati rice.

EGG CURRY

SERVES: 4–5
PREPARATION: 10 minutes
COOKING: 25–30 minutes

In every part of India a curry with hard boiled eggs is made by using the most common style curry. The variations of egg curry in India include Punjabi egg masala, simple egg gravy, egg butter masala, kadai egg masala, egg vindaloo, egg butter masala and many others. This simple egg curry recipe is the perfect way to start.

INGREDIENTS

- 6 cage free eggs—hardboiled and peeled
- 2 large yellow onions—diced
- 2 large tomatoes—diced
- 3 teaspoons coriander powder
- 1 teaspoon chili powder
- 1 teaspoon fennel seeds
- 1 teaspoon cumin seeds
- ½ teaspoon turmeric powder
- 2 teaspoons coconut powder
- 2 tablespoons cooking oil
- 1 tablespoon fresh lime juice
- 1 can coconut milk
- 1 cup water
- 1 cup quality cooking oil
- Salt to taste

METHOD

- Boil, cool, and peel the eggs. Then cut them in half, length-wise and set aside.

- In a heavy pot, heat 2 tablespoons of cooking oil to medium-high and cook the onions until golden brown or translucent, approximately 8-10 minutes. Then add the tomatoes, coriander powder, chili powder, fennel seeds, turmeric powder, coconut powder, 1 cup of water, salt to taste and cover the pot and turn the heat down to a simmer for 20 minutes. Stir occasionally.

- After 20 minutes, add the coconut milk and bring to a boil. Once at a boil, add the lime juice and then reduce the heat again to a low simmer.

- Do not add the eggs until ready for serving because the eggs will get mushy and fall apart sitting in the curry.

- When ready for serving, gently lay the boiled eggs with the yellow facing upwards. Carefully scoop into a serving dish.

EGG BHURJI

SERVES: 6
PREPARATION: 10 minutes
COOKING: 15 minutes

Scrambled eggs with herbs and spices

INGREDIENTS

- 12 cage free eggs
- ½ cup whole organic milk
- 3 large yellow onions—diced
- 2 large tomatoes—diced
- 2 bunches cilantro—finely chopped
- 2 green chillies—diced
- 1 tablespoon garlic-ginger paste
- ½ tablespoon black pepper powder
- ½ cup quality cooking oil
- Salt to taste

METHOD

- In a large bowl, whisk the 12 eggs with the milk and set aside. Do not add salt at this point because the salt will tend to make the eggs runny when they cook.

- In a large saucepan, heat 2 tablespoons of oil to medium heat. Add the onions and cook for 6-8 minutes, stirring occasionally, until just translucent. Once translucent, add the tomatoes, green chillies, garlic-ginger paste and black pepper. Stir the pan vigorously.

- Add the beaten egg mixture to the pan, stir quickly incorporating all the ingredients with the eggs. Keep stirring vigorously, scraping around the edges in order to cook all the egg. It is important to infuse air into the eggs by stirring vigorously the entire time the eggs are cooking. But, do not overcook the eggs. They should be fluffy, not hard.

- Add the salt and cilantro at the very last minute before removing the eggs from the heat and stir well. Remove from heat right after stirring as the cilantro should be as fresh as possible.

- Quickly transfer onto a serving dish. Serve with buttered toast for breakfast.

FISH TAMATAR

SERVES: 4
PREPARATION: 30 minutes marination; thereafter 30 minutes
COOKING: 30–35 minutes

Fish cooked in thick tomato puree

INGREDIENTS

- 2 pounds sole fish fillets
- 3 large tomatoes—chopped
- 1 bunch cilantro—chopped
- 1 teaspoon chopped cashew nuts
- 1 teaspoon chili powder
- 1 tablespoon coconut powder
- 1 teaspoon garam masala
- 1 teaspoon garlic-ginger paste
- 1 teaspoon sunflower seeds
- ¼ cup heavy cream
- 1 tablespoon fresh lemon juice
- ½ cup quality cooking oil
- Salt to taste

METHOD

- In a large bowl, marinate the fish in a mixture of the garlic-ginger paste, salt, lemon juice, and half of the chili powder. Set aside for 30 minutes.
- In a blender, grind the coconut powder, sunflower seeds and cashew nuts with a little water to make a paste.
- In a sauté pan, heat the cooking oil to a medium-high. Once hot, carefully add the fish and sauté lightly until golden brown on each side. Once done, set aside on a plate. In the remaining oil, add the tomatoes and stir in salt, the other half of the chili powder and cook for 5 minutes.
- Take the tomato gravy from the pan and strain it.
- Pour it back in a pot on medium heat and add the coconut, sunflower seeds and cashew nut paste, cook for 5 minutes, stirring constantly.
- Then, add the garam masala, the fried fish and heavy cream, let simmer for 3-4 minutes until the fish is well done.
- Garnish with chopped cilantro.

GREEN CHICKEN CURRY

SERVES: 4
PREPARATION: 30 minutes
COOKING: 40 minutes

My Mom used to make this for us and we call it Rus Chawal—"curry rice".

INGREDIENTS

- 1 pound skinless, boneless chicken—cut into 2 inch pieces
- 1 large yellow onion—chopped
- 1 tablespoon garlic-ginger paste
- 2 bunches cilantro—chopped
- 1 ounce cashew nuts—chopped
- 1 tablespoon poppy seeds
- 5 tablespoons unsweetened coconut powder
- 5 green chillies
- 3 green cardamoms
- 1 teaspoon cumin seeds
- 2 tablespoons coriander powder
- 1 teaspoon sugar
- 1 tablespoon turmeric water (turmeric dissolved in water)
- 4 teaspoons fresh lime juice
- ½ cup quality cooking oil
- 2 cups water
- Salt to taste

METHOD

- In a blender, grind together the poppy seeds, coconut powder, chillies, onions, garlic-ginger paste, cashew nuts and cardamom and set aside.

- Separately puree the cilantro. Add a bit of water to make the consistency of the cilantro as a puree. Set aside.

- Take the coriander powder and mix it with a little water to make a paste.

- In a medium sauté pan, heat the cooking oil to medium-high and add the cumin seeds. When the cumin seeds begin to fry, add the coriander paste and the spice paste and cook for 10 minutes, stirring constantly.

- After 10 minutes, add the chicken pieces, pureed cilantro-spice paste, sugar, salt and water and bring to a boil. Once it reaches a boil, reduce the heat to a simmer and cook the chicken until tender (approximately 10-15 minutes), stirring occasionally.

- Serve hot over Basmati rice.

KHEEMA CURRY

SERVES: 6
PREPARATION: 20 minutes
COOKING: 1 hour

Minced lamb with green peas and potato. Any type of meat can be used in the preparation of kheema.

INGREDIENTS

- 1 pound minced lamb
- 2 large yellow onions—diced
- 2 large Yukon potatoes—diced
- 4 large tomatoes—skinned and diced
- 2 bunches cilantro—finely chopped
- 1 pound green peas
- 1 teaspoon garlic-ginger paste
- 1 teaspoon turmeric powder
- 1 teaspoon garam masala
- 3 teaspoons fresh lime juice
- 1 cup quality cooking oil
- Salt to taste

METHOD

- In a large pot or wok, heat the oil to medium-high and add the onions. Cook the onions until golden brown and translucent.

- In another pan, on medium heat, fry the diced potatoes until lightly brown and just tender.

- Boil the green peas to just underdone. Do not over boil or the peas will separate from their skins and become mushy.

- Add the minced lamb, chopped tomatoes, garlic-ginger paste, turmeric powder, garam masala, and salt to the fried onions and allow to cook over a very low heat for 10 minutes. Then add four cups of water and allow to reduce over low heat until most of the water has evaporated and the lamb is soft and tender.

- Once the lamb is soft and tender, add the par boiled green peas, lightly fried potatoes and lime juice to the mixture.

- Garnish with cilantro and serve.

KERA-PER-EDA
(EGGS ON FRIED BANANAS)

SERVES: 6
PREPARATION: 10 minutes
COOKING: 25 minutes

As a child, our 90 year-old neighbor would make this dish and call me over to eat with her. It is one of my favorites.

INGREDIENTS

- 6 cage free eggs
- 6 ripe plantains (bananas)
- 2 tablespoons nutmeg powder
- 2 tablespoons raisins
- 2 tablespoons rose water
- 2 tablespoons sugar
- ½ cup quality cooking oil
- Salt to taste

METHOD

- Take the unpeeled plantains and lightly roll each to loosen from the skin. Peel and slice them in small discs.

- In a large frying pan, with a clear cover (preferably), heat 2 tablespoons of cooking oil on high heat and add the banana slices, fry until soft and golden. Remove from pan and mash the cooked bananas until soft, mix in the sugar, nutmeg powder, raisins and rose water. Spread the smashed bananas back into the same frying pan.

- Make 6 shallow holes in the banana mixture and heat the pan to low. Sprinkle 2 tablespoons of water over the bananas. When the banana pancake becomes warm crack 1 egg at a time in a saucer and then gentle pour the egg into each banana hole. After all the eggs have been used, sprinkle a little salt over the eggs, cover and cook until the eggs are solid—approximately 3-5 minutes. You are basically poaching the eggs in the mixture, so a medium-low heat is essential.

- Once the white of the eggs sets up and becomes opaque/milky white and the yokes look slightly set, remove the pan from the heat. It would be best if you have a frying pan with a see-through cover so that you can see if the egg whites are set up, otherwise you will have to remove the cover and that lets the steam out thus increasing the time needed to poach the eggs. Try not to remove the cover until ready.

- Serve immediately with hot toast.

FRIED BROWN RICE

SERVES: 4
PREPARATION: 15 minutes for soaking; thereafter 5 minutes
COOKING: 35–45 minutes

This rice is specific and special rice that is always served with Dhanshak Dal and meat kebab.

INGREDIENTS

- 1 pound raw Basmati rice
- 2 large yellow onions—thinly sliced
- 1 cinnamon stick
- 2 pieces bay leaf
- 2 teaspoons sugar
- 4 cups water
- 5 tablespoons quality cooking oil
- Salt to taste

METHOD

- Soak the uncooked rice for 15 minutes. Wash well and drain.

- In a deep pot, heat cooking oil to medium and fry the onions until golden brown and translucent. Then, add the cinnamon stick, bay leaves and sauté for 5 minutes. Add the sugar and let it caramelize. Stir constantly so that the sugar doesn't sit and burn.

- Once the sugar has melted and becomes a light golden, add the rice and sauté for 3 minutes. Then add 4 cups of water, salt to taste and cook for 10 minutes covered until the water has boiled off and the rice is cooked through.

- Serve with hot Dhanshak Dal (see recipe on pg. 195).

KOLMI–NO–PATIO

SERVES: 6–8
PREPARATION: 20 minutes
COOKING: 45-50 minutes

A patio (pronounced: pah-thi-o) is a parsi style prawn curry with sweet, hot and sour flavors equally balanced. Parsi's serve the patio on auspicious family occasions, along with white rice, yellow lentils, and calling it by its traditional name DHANDAR-NI-PATIO (dal with red sauce).

INGREDIENTS

- 20-30 king prawns (jumbo shrimp)— peeled and deveined
- 2 large yellow onions—chopped
- 4 large tomatoes—chopped
- 1 eggplant—cut into bit sized pieces
- 4 bunches cilantro-chopped
- 4 curry leaves
- 4 green chillies—slit in half
- ½ cup white vinegar
- ½ cup of crushed jaggery
  (jaggery is a course dark brown sugar made from evaporated palm tree sap—it tastes like brown sugar and caramel. You can buy this from any Indian food store)
- 12 large red dry chillies
- ½ cup unsweetened coconut powder
- 2 tablespoons cumin seeds
- 2 tablespoons garlic-ginger paste
- 1 tablespoon mustard seeds
- 1 tablespoon parsi dhansakh masala (available in Indian grocery store)
- 1 ½ cups quality cooking oil
- Salt to taste

METHOD

- Wash shrimp, apply salt all over each shrimp piece and set aside.

- In a deep heavy-bottomed pan heat to medium-high ½ cup cooking oil. Once hot, add onions and curry leaves and allow the leaves to crackle. Cook the onions until they are golden brown, translucent and soft—approximately 10 minutes.

- In a mixer, finely grind the following spices:
  - Red dry chillies
  - Coconut powder
  - Cumin seeds
  - Garlic-ginger paste
  - Mustard seeds
  - Parsi dhansakh masala
  - 3 bunches of cilantro

- To the onions, add the chopped tomatoes, the ground spices and slit green chillies and cook over low heat for 20 minutes. Stir well.

- After 20 minutes, add the shrimp and cooked them over a low heat. Add 2 cups of water, the vinegar and the crushed jaggery. Simmer for 5 minutes or until the shrimp turns a bright pink. Do not overcook the shrimp. Once done, take off the heat and set aside.

- In another pan, over medium-high heat, add 1 cup of cooking oil and fry the eggplant. When the eggplant pieces are golden brown on all sides, use a slotted spoon and set aside on a paper towel to soak up any access oil.

- Decorate the patio with the fried eggplant and remaining cilantro.

- Serve with Basmati rice.

LAMB JARDALOO SALLI BOTI

SERVES: 6–8
PREPARATION: 30 minutes for soaking; thereafter 45 minutes
COOKING: 3 hours

Sweet and sour lamb cooked with apricots and shoe string potatoes. A classic Parsi dish. Jardaloo means dried apricot, boti means small pieces of meat, salli means potato shoe strings.

INGREDIENTS

- 4 pounds boneless lamb—cubed
- 5 large yellow onions—diced
- 4 large tomatoes—boiled, skinned and finely chopped (can use canned tomatoes)
- 20 pieces dried apricots
- 1 cup quality red vinegar
- ½ cup sugar
- ½ cup water and 4 cups of water
- Salli (potato shoestrings)—available in any grocery store
- 2 teaspoons garam masala powder
- ½ teaspoon chili powder
- ½ teaspoon turmeric powder
- ½ teaspoon black pepper
- 3 tablespoons golden raisins
- 3 tablespoons cashew nuts
- 1 tablespoon garlic-ginger paste
- Quality cooking oil
- Salt to taste

METHOD

- In a bowl, mix the vinegar, sugar and water. Wash the dried apricots and then soak them in the vinegar mixture for 30 minutes.
- In a large sauté pan or wok, heat cooking oil to medium and add the onions. Cook them until golden brown and translucent.
- In a cooking pot, add the lamb with garlic-ginger paste, garam masala, chili powder, turmeric powder, black pepper, and tomatoes, stir and cook on low heat for 10 minutes.
- After 10 minutes, add the 4 cups of water and cook until the lamb is tender, this will take two to three hours on a gas fire. Keep adding water until the meat is tender. Keep the heat on low.
- When the meat is tender add in the apricot mixture, cook for 5 minutes and then remove the pot from the fire.
- Right before service, sprinkle raisins, cashew nuts, potato shoestrings (salli) and cilantro.

MARGHI-NA-FARCHA

SERVES: 4
PREPARATION: 30 minutes for marination; thereafter 15 minutes
COOKING: 20 minutes

Parsi fried (farcha) chicken (marghi) is usually served as a starter at all types of festivities. Amongst Parsis, it is a must at all gatherings.

INGREDIENTS

- 8 pieces skin-on chicken bone (leg quarter)
- 4 cage free eggs
- 2 pieces green chillies—diced
- 1 bunch cilantro—chopped
- ½ stalk celery—chopped
- 1 ½ teaspoons garlic-ginger paste
- 1 ½ teaspoons chili paste
- ¾ teaspoon turmeric powder
- ½ teaspoon cinnamon powder
- ½ teaspoon clove powder
- ½ teaspoon black pepper
- 2 cups unseasoned bread crumbs
- 1 cup quality cooking oil
- 1 cup water
- Salt to taste

METHOD

- Wash the chicken well, leaving the skin on. Dry well and place in a large bowl. Add the salt, garlic-ginger paste, chili powder, turmeric powder, cinnamon powder, clove powder and black pepper. Mix well so as to coat the chicken pieces all over. Make sure you either wear kitchen disposable gloves or wash your hands very well after mixing because of the chili powder and raw chicken. Do not rub your face while mixing. Cover the chicken and allow to marinate for at least 30 minutes.

- Place the chicken in a heavy bottomed pan along with the green chillies, celery and cilantro and 1 cup of water. On a low heat, simmer until the flesh is soft and tender, then, remove from the fire.

- In a large, heavy-bottomed stock pot or Dutch oven, heat the cooking oil over medium-high heat (approximately 360 degrees).

- In a medium-sized bowl, beat the 4 eggs and dip each chicken piece in the beaten eggs. Then coat each piece thoroughly with the bread crumbs.

- When the oil is ready, carefully place 4-5 pieces of chicken in the oil and fry until golden brown all over. Be sure the chicken is not pink inside. If so, make sure the oil is hot and fry another 2 minutes, or until there is no pink inside. Once done, place the fried chicken on laid out paper towels over a baking sheet or plate and let sit for a minute to absorb any excess oil.

- Serve hot.

MUTTON KEBAB

SERVES: 6–8
PREPARATION: 2 hours
COOKING: 40–50 minutes

This is a dish that my Mom used to make along with our traditional Parsi dhanshak every Sunday.

INGREDIENTS

- 1 pound minced lamb
- 4 large Yukon potatoes—cooked and mashed
- 2 large yellow onions—chopped
- 3-4 green chillies—minced
- 4 cage-free eggs
- 1 cup unseasoned bread crumbs
- 2 bunches cilantro—chopped
- 3 teaspoons mint—chopped
- 2 teaspoons turmeric powder
- 1 teaspoon garlic-ginger paste
- 1 teaspoon chili powder
- 1 teaspoon garam masala
- Quality frying oil
- Salt to taste

METHOD

- In a big bowl, combine the minced lamb, mashed potatoes, onions, cilantro, mint, green chili, turmeric powder, garlic-ginger paste, chili powder, garam masala and salt. Mix well and form medium-sized round balls with your hands.
- In a medium bowl, beat the 4 eggs.
- Take a flat plate and spread the bread crumbs.
- Dip the balls in the beaten egg, and then roll around in the bread crumbs. Set each ball aside on a plate.
- In a medium heavy-bottomed pot or Dutch oven, heat the frying oil to medium-high. When the oil is hot, fry the mutton balls in batches of 6 to 8, turning once, cooking until golden brown. Carefully remove with a wire strainer and transfer to prepared paper towels on a sheet pan.

PARSI PORO (OMELET)

SERVES: 5
PREPARATION: 10 minutes
COOKING: 15 minutes

Omelets are made by people all over the world, and the variations are almost infinite. Our Parsi poro (omelet) is not only a breakfast favorite, but can be turned into a delicious omelet sandwich with melted cheese. My Mom used to make this omelet for our picnics. She would serve it with sliced buttered bread and fresh orange marmalade.

INGREDIENTS

- 8 cage free eggs
- 2 large yellow onions—diced
- 1 bunch cilantro—finely chopped
- 1 tablespoon mint—minced
- 3 green chillies—deseeded and minced
- ½ teaspoon garlic—minced
- ½ teaspoon turmeric powder
- ½ teaspoon ground white pepper
- 1 teaspoon chili powder
- ½ cup cooking oil
- Salt to taste

METHOD

- In a large mixing bowl, combine the eggs, cilantro, mint, chillies, garlic, turmeric, white pepper, chili powder and salt to taste. Set aside.

- You can choose to cook the onions prior to adding to the egg mixture if you prefer a sweeter, translucent onion. Traditionally, however, we do not pre-cook the onion prior to cooking it in the omelet. We add the raw diced onion to the egg mixture.

- In a nonstick pan, heat 1 tablespoon of oil to medium heat. Allow it to heat well, stir the egg mixture and pour ¼ of it in the pan. Allow the underside to become golden brown and then flip it over and cook the other side over medium heat. If the heat is too intense when you pour the egg mixture the omelet will burn and turn out raw.

- You can make 5 omelets out of this mixture and serve them with fresh squeezed lime and buttered toast.

- A nice alternate omelet is adding cheese. When you flip the omelet to cook the second side, then add the cheese of your choice to the cooked side and fold the omelet in half to melt the cheese.

PATRA-NI-MACHHI

SERVES: 6–8
PREPARATION: 15–20 minutes
COOKING: 30 minutes

Patra-Ni-Machhi is fish with chutney wrapped in banana leaves. "Machhi" means fish, and "patra" means leaves. The white/silver pomfret, which is required for this dish, looks pale grey to white, is flat shaped and has white meat that is similar in taste to Tilapia. It is found in the Atlantic, Indian and Pacific Oceans. This fish delight is always served as one of many tasty dishes at a Parsi wedding.

INGREDIENTS

- 2 large Pomfrets, each cut into 5 slices
- 1 cup unsweetened coconut powder
- 1 bunch cilantro—chopped
- 6 green chillies—diced
- 2 teaspoons garlic-ginger paste
- 1 cup mint—chopped
- 10 black peppercorns
- 1 tablespoon cumin seeds
- 2 tablespoons fresh lemon juice
- 2 tablespoons sugar
- 6 large banana leaves (very soft) (available in Indian grocery store)
- ½ cup white vinegar
- ½ cup water
- ½ cup quality cooking oil
- Salt to taste
- Thread for wrapping

METHOD

- Wash the Pomfrets very well (usually twice), apply salt all over each and set aside.

- **MINT-CILANTRO CHUTNEY**: Put the coconut powder into a blender with the chopped cilantro, garlic-ginger paste, green chillies, peppercorns, cumin seeds, lemon juice, sugar and salt. Grind, use ½ cup of water if necessary to make into a pureed pulp.

- Prepare the banana leaves by washing thoroughly and removing the center stalk. You will have twelve banana leaves now. Take 1 piece of fish at a time and smother it with the chutney. It should be well coated. Then wrap each piece of fish in 1 piece of banana leaf. Wrap each of them as tight as you can without tearing the leaf. The wrapping doesn't have to be extremely tight, just snug enough to hold the fish, the chutney and the cooking juice inside while it steams. Secure the wrapped fish inside the banana leaf with a thin thread (see picture).

- When all the slices are neatly packed, take a deep pot and add water and vinegar and heat to medium-high. Once hot, carefully arrange the banana leaf fish packages in the water and cover tightly. Then reduce the heat to low and cook for 15 minutes. Half way through the cooking, turn over the packages and finish cooking.

- Once steamed, carefully remove the packages from the water and place on a tray lined with a kitchen towel to catch the moisture from the packages. Let sit for 1 minute and then serve.

- **TO SERVE:** Cut the thread holding the package together, and serve the entire banana leaf fish package on the plate.

TARELI MACHI

SERVES: 6
PREPARATION: 30 minutes marination; thereafter 20 minutes
COOKING: 25 minutes

Parsi style fried fish. The pomfret fish that I refer to in this recipe is also known as the Paplet in Bombay and is called either silver or white pomfret, of the genus pampus argenteus (aka butterfish). It is easily found on the west coast of India in the states of Maharashtra and Gujarat. It is a white meat fish similar in taste and texture to Tilapia. One can find pomfret in any local Asian market.

INGREDIENTS

- 2 white/silver Pomfret (fish), each cut into three pieces
- 2 teaspoons chili powder
- 1 teaspoon turmeric powder
- ½ teaspoon coriander powder
- ½ teaspoon black pepper powder
- Salt to taste
- Quality cooking oil as needed

METHOD

- In a large bowl, combine the chili powder, turmeric powder, coriander powder, black powders and salt.
- Wash fish pieces well, pat dry and coat them in the spice mixture. Cover, and allow them to sit in the mixture for at least 30 minutes.
- Take a large nonstick pan or a round tava (Indian style wok) and heat cooking oil on high. When the oil is hot, carefully place each piece of fish into the oil and fry quickly. The fish pieces should harden on the outside like a normal fish batter. All you want is a light fry in order to cook the delicate fish meat. You want the fish meat to stay soft and buttery. As the outside turns a bit golden, take out the fish and place on paper towels in order to absorb any oil.
- Serve hot with lemon wedges and mint chutney.

CHUTNEYS & RELISHES

(Chatanee Aur Svaad)

MINT CHUTNEY

SPICY RED CHUTNEY

TAMARIND CHUTNEY

CABBAGE SALAD

KACHUMBAR SALAD

PEACH CHUTNEY

YOGURT RAITA

No Indian meal is complete without at least one kind of relish. There are so many different kinds of chutneys, sweet chutney, sour chutney, hot chutney.

The ingredients used in chutney can include tomatoes, ginger, garlic-ginger paste, onions, tamarind, coconut, fresh cilantro, fresh mint, lime juice, yogurt, dates, salt to taste. Chutneys are generally served in a small quantity to accompany a meal or appetizers.

MINT CHUTNEY

SERVES: 6–10
PREPARATION: 20 minutes
No cooking time

Mint, cilantro, chili blended together with a touch of fresh lemon juice

INGREDIENTS

- 1 small yellow onion—roughly chopped
- ¾ cup cilantro
- 2 tablespoons mint leaves
- 1 cup grated coconut
- 6 deseeded green chillies
- 1 teaspoon cumin seeds
- 1 ½ teaspoons sugar
- 2 teaspoons fresh lemon juice
- Salt to taste

METHOD

- In a blender, combine all the ingredients except the lemon juice and sugar (do not add water). When the mixture is like a thick puree, add the sugar and lemon juice. Blend for another minute.
- Serve with any appetizers.

SPICY RED CHUTNEY

SERVES: 15–20
PREPARATION: 30 minutes
No cooking time

A delicious spicy tomato based chutney

INGREDIENTS

- 2 pounds red tomatoes
- ½ cup yellow onion—rough chop
- 2 tablespoons fresh garlic
- 2 tablespoons chili powder
- 1 teaspoon paprika powder
- 2 tablespoons white vinegar
- 6 green chillies
- Salt to taste

METHOD

- Boil the tomatoes in a pot for 5 minutes. After 5 minutes, drain the water, and let the tomatoes cool before handling. Once cool, peel, deseed and chop the tomatoes into large pieces.

- In a large sauce pot, over medium-high heat, combine the vinegar, salt, and 1 cup of water. When the mixture starts bubbling add the onions, garlic, chili powder, paprika powder, and green chillies. Cook until the mixture thickens, approximately 5-8 minutes, stirring constantly.

- Once the mixture thickens, remove from the heat and place it in a blender. Be careful as the mixture will be hot. Blend it for 5 minutes. Take a taste sample and if necessary, add 1 more tablespoon of vinegar to suit your preference for the sour balance with the heat of the chili. Let the mixture cool and place in a jar or bowl that can be covered.

- Refrigerate until use.

TAMARIND CHUTNEY

SERVES: 4
PREPARATION: 30 minutes
COOKING: 40 minutes

Sweet and sour chutney with tamarind and honey dates

INGREDIENTS

- 10 pieces pitted honey dates
- 1 cup tamarind pulp
  (Tamarind pulp can be found in any Indian/Asian market or online. It is sold compressed and very dense. Do not confuse it with tamarind paste, which is tamarind pulp without the seeds and fibers. For the chutney you will need the pulp because of the concentration of flavor and density)
- ½ cup sugar
- 1 teaspoon chili powder
- ½ teaspoon cumin powder
- 1 cup water
- Salt to taste

METHOD

- In a medium saucepan, combine honey dates, tamarind, sugar, chili powder, cumin powder, and salt with 1 cup of water and bring it to a fast boil. Stir continuously.

- Once the contents start boiling, turn the heat down to a simmer and cook for 15 minutes. After 15 minutes, place the mixture in a blender and blend for 5 minutes. Be careful as the mixture will be hot.

- Once blended, remove from blender and place in a bottle or bowl and chill in the refrigerator until ready for use.

CABBAGE SALAD

SERVES: 4
PREPARATION: 30 minutes

Cabbage with roasted cumin seeds, mustard seed, white lentils. This is my signature salad at my California restaurants.

INGREDIENTS

- ½ cabbage—chopped
- 2 tablespoons cumin seeds
- 2 tablespoons mustard seed
- 2 tablespoon white udit dal
- 4 tablespoons fresh lemon juice
- 3 tablespoons high quality extra virgin olive oil
- Salt to taste

METHOD

- In a large bowl, add the chopped cabbage. Set aside.
- In a deep soup ladle heat the olive oil over a medium flame. If you don't have an open flame burner, then in a small sauce pot, heat the olive oil over a medium-high heat. When the oil gets hot, add the mustard seeds, cumin seeds, and white lentil. They will start to pop from the hot oil. When they pop, wait 30 seconds and then remove the oil from the heat. Pour the hot mixture into a large mixing bowl where the chopped cabbage has been sitting. Add the lemon juice and salt to taste, mix well.
- Transfer to a serving dish. Can be served chilled or warm.

KACHUMBAR (SALAD)

SERVES: 4–6
PREPARATION: 20 minutes

My Mom use to serve this salad with dhansak.

INGREDIENTS

- 2 large yellow onions—diced
- 4 tomatoes—diced
- ½ cucumber—peeled, deseeded and diced
- 1 fresh green chili—diced
- ½ cup cilantro—finely chopped
- 4-5 fresh limes
- Salt and pepper to taste.

METHOD

- Deseeding cucumbers is done by slicing the cucumbers in half or in ¼ slices, then run the curved part of a spoon along the seed channel and scoop out.
- In a mixing bowl, combine the onions, tomatoes, cucumber, green chili, cilantro, lime juice, salt and pepper to taste and mix well.
- Serve with any entrée and with the remaining limes on the side.

PEACH CHUTNEY

SERVES: 15–20
PREPARATION: 30 minutes

Chunks of peach with a sweet and sour taste

INGREDIENTS

- 1 pound peaches—raw and diced
- 4 tablespoons apple cider vinegar
- ¾ cup sugar
- 5 cardamom pods
- ½ teaspoon coriander seeds—crushed
- ½ teaspoon onion seeds
- ½ teaspoon dried red chillies
- 1 piece fresh ginger—grated
- Salt to taste

METHOD

- In a medium sauce pan, heat the vinegar over a low heat and add the diced peaches, cover and cook for 15 minutes. After 15 minutes, add the chillies, onion seeds, salt and sugar, stir well. Simmer until the flavors of the spices infuse into the vinegar, another 10 minutes.

- After 10 minutes, add the grated ginger and bring to a boil, stirring constantly. Once it comes to a boil, turn the heat down to a simmer and cook until the peaches are soft and most of the vinegar has evaporated.

- Once the peaches are soft, remove from the heat and leave to cool. Give it a good stir before you leave it to cool.

- When cool, pour into bottles or bowls with a cover.

- Let the peach chutney sit in the refrigerator for a few days before serving in order for the flavors to marry.

YOGURT RAITA

SERVES: 10
PREPARATION: 30 minutes

An Indian yogurt dip/condiment that cools the palate to balance the spicy dishes.

INGREDIENTS

- 1 large cucumber—peeled, deseeded and diced
- 1 ½ cups plain organic whole yogurt
- ½ cup grape tomatoes—sliced or diced (to your preference)
- ½ teaspoon cumin powder
- ½ teaspoon sugar
- ½ teaspoon paprika powder
- ½ cup cilantro—finely chopped
- 1 green chili—minced (optional to taste)
- Salt to taste

METHOD

- To deseed the cucumber, slice it in half, or in ¼ slices, then run the scoop part of a spoon down the seed channel and scoop out.
- In a large bowl, beat the yogurt with a fork until smooth. Then add the cucumber, cumin powder, sugar, paprika powder, chili and salt, and mix well. Garnish with cilantro and tomato before serving.
- Goes very well with any spicy dish as the yogurt is cooling to the palate.

INDIAN DESSERTS & DRINKS

FALOODA

GAJAR HALWA

GULAB JAMUN

KHEER

KHOYA

LAGAN-NU-CUSTARD

MANGO ICE CREAM

MANGO MOUSSE

PARSI SEV

MASALA CHAI

MANGO LASSI

SWEET LASSI

In India most meals end with dessert, the art of making delicious sweets and desserts is known by special sweet makers (HALWAIS). These are simple recipes of what we serve in our restaurant. Most of the other sweets are served mainly at religious festivals and there are special shops in Mumbai that exclusively serve Indian desserts or sweets.

Indian sweets tend to be very sweet, most recipes use carrots, cottage cheese, pistachios, almonds, coconut, flours, sugar and the most important—milk. Milk forms the base of more than half of our sweets. Milk is boiled for hours until it forms a semi-solid dough called Khoya.

FALOODA

SERVES: 16 glasses
PREPARATION: 10 minutes
COOKING: 40 minutes

Falooda is a popular Indian cold drink dessert. It's unique ingredients of rose syrup, vermicelli (made from wheat), ice cream and fruit make it a rich and satisfying Indian sundae.

INGREDIENTS

- ½ cup falooda sev
  (available at any Indian grocery store)
- 1 bottle rose syrup
  (available at any Indian grocery store)
- 1 quart quality vanilla ice cream
- 2 liters whole organic milk
- 2 cups sugar
- ¼ cup black tukmaria seeds
  (tukmaria seeds are also known as basil seeds and can be found at any Indian grocery market or online)
- 5 tablespoons dried wheat milk powder
- ½ cup crushed pistachio nuts
- Optional: Rose petals for garnish

METHOD

- Soak the tukmaria seeds in 1 cup of water the day before and place it in the refrigerator.

- Before you start cooking the wheat milk, have a bowl filled with ice water ready. Then, in a large pot over medium heat, combine the wheat milk with 2 cups of water and ½ cup of sugar. Stir well for 30 minutes until you get a thick glutinous gel.

- As soon as the wheat milk is cooked, place it in a colander and stir it with a ladle so that beads of wheat milk fall into the icy water and firm immediately.

- To serve the falooda take 16 glasses and place 1 teaspoon of swollen black tukmaria seeds in each glass. Then place 1 tablespoon of wheat milk beads over the seeds. Then fill 1 inch of rose syrup in every glass. Pour milk in the glass until it is three quarter full. Top with a scoop of ice cream and serve.

- Garnish with rose petals if preferred.

GAJAR HALWA

SERVES: 10–12
PREPARATION: 20 minutes
COOKING: 45 minutes to 1 hour

Shredded carrot pudding with dried fruits

INGREDIENTS

- 1 pound carrots—washed, peeled, shredded
- 3 cups whole organic milk
- ½ cup sugar
- 1 teaspoon cardamom powder
- ¼ teaspoon clove powder
- ¼ teaspoon nutmeg powder
- ¼ teaspoon cinnamon powder
- 2 tablespoons slivered almonds
- 2 ½ tablespoons golden raisins
- 2 ½ tablespoons cashew nuts
- ½ cup ghee

METHOD

- In a heavy bottomed pot, add milk and carrots and bring to a boil. After it comes to a boil, reduce the heat to low and continue stirring for 20 to 30 minutes until the carrots are soft.

- Once the carrots are soft, add the sugar, cardamom powder, clove powder, nutmeg powder, cinnamon powder and the ghee. Stir continuously until the carrot mixture (halwa) slowly starts separating from the ghee.

- Once the ghee separates, add the almonds and raisins and stir for a further 5 minutes.

- Serve hot or chilled, sprinkle cashew nuts before service.

GULAB JAMUN

SERVES: 6–8
PREPARATION: 20 minutes
COOKING: 3 hours

Gulab (flower) jamun (fruit) is a fried ball made from milk solids (khoya) and then soaked in a light syrup accented with cardamom and saffron.

INGREDIENTS

BALLS:

- 2 cups milk powder
- 4 tablespoons ghee/unsalted butter
- ½ cup all-purpose flour
- A pinch of baking soda (⅛ teaspoon)
- ¼ cup whole organic milk
- 1 tablespoon crushed pistachios or other favorite nut

SYRUP:

- 1 ½ cups water
- ½ teaspoon fresh lemon juice
- 1 cup sugar
- 3 tablespoons honey
- Few threads saffron
- 1 teaspoon rose water (available at any Indian grocery store or online)
- 3 pods cardamom—crushed

METHOD

SYRUP:

- In a pot, boil the water, then add the sugar, lemon juice and honey, stir well. The lemon juice is added to keep the syrup from solidifying when the syrup cools. Then, immediately reduce the heat to low and cook for another 10 minutes.
- After 10 minutes, turn off the heat. The syrup should be kept at a liquid consistency. If it should start to form strings add a couple drops of lemon juice and stir thoroughly until you get the liquid syrup (like maple syrup) consistency.
- Add the cardamom, saffron and rose water to the syrup, stir and keep the syrup in a warm place or on very low on the stove. The syrup needs to remain warm for the fried balls.

GULAB JAMUN BALLS:

- In a mixing bowl, combine the milk powder, baking soda, and flour. Then add the ¼ cup of whole milk (4 tablespoons) and 2 tablespoons of ghee. Mix well into a soft dough. If the dough is still crumbly/dry, add 1 teaspoon of ghee until you get a soft, almost sticky dough.
- **IMPORTANT:** Do not over mix/over knead the dough, otherwise, the gluten forms and the balls will become dense (instead of light and airy on the inside), thus, not being able to absorb the syrup.

- Make balls out of the dough (approximately 12-14). The dough tends to harden quickly, so fry the balls immediately. In a deep frying pan, heat the frying oil to medium-low (it is important that the temperature of the oil stay relatively low—about 298 degrees Fahrenheit—so that the balls cook thoroughly and not just brown from the outside while remaining raw inside). To test the oil:
Drop a small piece of the dough in the oil and if:
  - The dough comes to the surface without changing color, the oil is ready.
  - The dough comes to the surface and is brown, the oil is too hot, reduce the heat.
  - The dough doesn't come up, the oil is too cold and it needs to be heated.
- Slowly place each ball into the oil with a slotted spoon. Keep turning the balls and do not let them sit at the bottom of the pan. If the ball is allowed to sit with any side touching the pan while frying then that touching side won't fry properly and there will be a "raw" spot of white on an otherwise golden brown ball (see picture). The balls will expand in size while cooking. After 3 minutes the color of the balls will start to change light golden brown, then after another 5 minutes the balls will darken a bit to a golden brown.
- Remove with a slotted spoon to paper towels so that any excess oil is absorbed. After about 1 minute on the paper towels transfer the balls into the warm syrup. Let the balls sit in the syrup for at least 1.5 hours. Repeat this process for all the balls.
- They can be served chilled or warm.
  OPTIONAL: Garnish with crushed pistachios or other favorite nut.

KHEER

SERVES: 5–6
PREPARATION: 30 minutes
COOKING: 35–45 minutes

A dessert made with milk and rice. This is my mother's recipe, on special occasions she would make it early in the morning.

INGREDIENTS

- ¾ cup Basmati rice
- 4 cups whole organic milk
- 2 cups sugar
- 4 cardamom pods—crushed
- 10 pistachios-unsalted and crushed
- 1 tablespoon rose water
- OPTIONAL: ¼ cup raisins (preferably golden)
- Saffron threads for garnish

METHOD

- In a bowl, soak the uncooked rice in cold water for 30 minutes.
- After soaking, wash the rice thoroughly. Once washed, place the rice in a cooker or in a large pot. Add 4 cups of water to the rice and cook until done. Once done, mash the rice.
- In a heavy bottomed pot, add the milk, cardamom and sugar and bring to a boil, stirring constantly. Once the mixture starts to boil, add the rice, pistachios, and raisins and lower the heat to a simmer. Continue to cook for another 20-25 minutes until the mixture thickens.
- Once thick, remove from the heat and let cool. Then add the rose water and stir well.
- The kheer can be served cold or warm. Garnish with additional pistachios and saffron threads.

KHOYA (MAWA)

COOKING:
1 ½ hours—as necessary to burn down the milk into its solids

Khoya is concentrated milk solids reduced from whole milk. It is used as a base for most Indian desserts because it is rich, creamy and delicious. It is an Indian version of ricotta cheese.

INGREDIENTS

- 2 liters whole organic milk
  (the milk must be whole as the purpose is to burn down the milk to get just the creamy fat)

METHOD

- Boil the milk in a heavy bottomed pot until the milk looks like it will start to froth over. Then turn the heat down to low—stirring constantly and scrapping the sides of the pot and bottom until a thick paste forms.
- This paste is the base for most Indian desserts.

LAGAN—NU—CUSTARD

SERVES: 12–15
PREPARATION: 40 minutes
COOKING: 40–50 minutes

At every Parsi wedding, sweet and creamy custard is served with almond slices.

INGREDIENTS

- 3 liters whole organic milk
- ½ can condensed milk
- 6 cage free eggs—beaten
- 1-2 cups sugar (per taste)
- ½ cup slivered almonds
- ¼ cup unsalted pistachios—crushed
- ½ teaspoon cardamom powder
- ½ teaspoon nutmeg powder
- 1 tablespoon quality vanilla extract
- 1 stick unsalted butter

METHOD

- Boil the milk in a heavy bottomed pot. Once it comes to a boil, remove from the heat and stir in the condensed milk and sugar. Place the pot on the heat again and bring to a boil. Keep stirring for 25 minutes. After 25 minutes, remove from the heat and let cool.

- Preheat the oven at 350 degrees Fahrenheit.

- Lightly grease a baking dish with the butter.

- In a mixing bowl, beat the eggs, add the vanilla, cardamom, nutmeg and thoroughly mix that in to the eggs. Once all the ingredients are incorporated, pour this mixture into the cooled milk and whisk together for at least 2 minutes.

- Pour this mixture into the baking dish and bake at 350 degrees Fahrenheit for 35-40 or just until the top turns a golden brown and when you insert a toothpick in the center it comes out clean.

- Once baked, remove from the oven, top the dish with almonds and pistachios and then chill in the refrigerator for about 1 hour.

- When ready to serve, cut into slices and serve with whipped cream.

MANGO ICE CREAM

SERVES: 4–5
PREPARATION: 25 minutes
COOKING: 40 minutes

Homemade mango ice cream

INGREDIENTS

- 1 ¼ cups canned mango puree (found at any Indian or Asian market)
- ½ cup heavy cream
- 1 tablespoon fresh lemon juice
- ¼ teaspoon good vanilla extract
- ¼ cup sugar/honey (as preferred)
- 4 egg whites—beaten
- 1 cup condensed milk
- 1 cup chopped nuts of your choice
- A few strands of saffron
- 6–8 kulfi (ice cream) molds
- 6–8 wooden sticks for molds

METHOD

- Boil the condensed milk for 10 minutes. Then, add the mango pulp, puree, and stir vigorously. Cook further for another 2 minutes. Take it off the fire and put it on the side. Let cool completely.

- Beat the egg whites until frothy or they make small peaks.

- Mix the cooled mango mixture with the egg whites, vanilla extract, and heavy cream in a mixer. Lastly add the saffron threads and nuts and lightly mix in.

- Spoon the mixture into 6-8 ice cream/kulfi molds. Tightly seal the molds insert sticks with plastic wrap or a sealable top and freeze for at least 40 minutes, (it depends on how hard one desires it)

- Shake the mold three times during the first hour of freezing.

- Just prior to serving, dip the bottom of the molds in hot water just for a few seconds to loosen the sides.

MANGO MOUSSE

SERVES: 6

PREPARATION: 4 hours for setting; 20 minutes preparation

INGREDIENTS

- 2 medium sized mangoes—cubed
- ½ cup heavy cream
- 1 tablespoon honey or sugar (to your preference)
- 2 teaspoon fresh lime or lemon juice (your preference)
- 2 egg whites
- 1 pinch of salt

METHOD

- Peel and remove the flesh from the mangoes. Puree the mango pulp and lime/lemon juice in a blender.
- Beat the egg whites with the salt until they are frothy making small peaks when you pull the whites up with the beater.
- Sprinkle in the sugar and continue to beat the whites. Then gently hand-fold the heavy cream into the whites. Do not over mix as the air that was built into the whites will be beaten out.
- Gradually fold the mango puree into the egg white mixture.
- Carefully, spoon the mixture into serving glasses or bowl, chill for at least 4 hours before service.
- Garnish with mango pieces and some minced mint leaves

PARSI SEV (SWEET VERMICELLI)

SERVES: 5–6
PREPARATION: 35 minutes
COOKING: 35–45 minutes

This is a sweet dish prepared on special days and celebrations. My mother-in-law makes a version that tastes just like pumpkin pie.

INGREDIENTS

- 1 packet vermicelli
  (available in any Indian grocery store)
  (break the uncooked vermicelli up into little pieces)
- 1 ½ cups sugar
- 1 ½ cups ghee (pure clarified butter)
- ½ cup almonds—slivered
- ½ cup raisins
- 1 teaspoon quality vanilla extract
- 1 cup water

METHOD

- Heat ½ cup ghee in a frying pan on medium-high heat and add almonds and raisins and sauté for 2 minutes or until very light brown, remove from the heat and set aside.

- Heat 1 cup water in a pot then add sugar and stir for 5 minutes so that the sugar dissolves completely. Once dissolved, set pot aside.

- In a sauté pan, heat on low, 1 cup of ghee and add the broken vermicelli. Cook gently, stirring lightly but continuously so that the strands of vermicelli do not burn. When the vermicelli becomes light brown, add the sugar water, vanilla and then bring the mixture to a quick boil.

- Once the mixture starts to boil, reduce the heat to low, cover the pan and cook the remaining liquid off. The vermicelli will absorb the water and become like soft noodles.

- Serve hot on a plate and garnish with almond and raisins.

MASALA CHAI

Serves: 8–10
Preparation: 15 minutes

Indian tea steeped in spices and milk

INGREDIENTS

- 12 pieces clove
- 6 cardamom pods
- 1 cinnamon stick
- 1 (¼ inch) piece ginger root, peeled and thinly sliced
- 3 cups whole organic milk (it depends how strong you want it)
- 4 tablespoons black tea powder, (high quality, preferably Darjeeling tea)
- 6 cups water

METHOD

- In a pot or kettle, boil the water.
- Add the cinnamon stick, clove, cardamom, and ginger. Boil for 5 minutes. Once boiled, reduce the heat to a simmer and add milk, black tea powder and let simmer for 10 minutes.
- Strain the mixture and serve hot.
- If needed, serve with the sugar.

SWEET LASSI

Serves: 4
Preparation: 10 minutes

Lassi is a very popular yogurt based drink. Because of the live cultures in yogurt, this drink is traditionally used after a spicy meal to cool the stomach and help the intestinal tract.

INGREDIENTS

- 1 cup organic plain whole yogurt; can substitute thicker yogurt for a thicker drink, such as Greek or cream-top yogurt
- 1 cup whole organic milk
- 1 tablespoon sugar to taste

METHOD

- Place the yogurt in a blender and whisk it for about 2 minutes then add milk and sugar to taste and continue to whisk for another 2-3 minutes.
- Pour the Lassi into a serving glass.
- Served chilled.

MANGO LASSI

INGREDIENTS

- ½ can of mango pulp

METHOD

- Use the same method as sweet Lassi, but, add mango pulp in it and whisk for 2 minutes before pouring into a glass.

CONVERSION GUIDE

These are not exact equivalents; they've been rounded-off to make measuring easier

DRY MEASURES

METRIC	IMPERIAL
15 g	½ oz
30 g	1 oz
60 g	2 oz
90 g	3 oz
125 g	4 oz (¼ lb)
155 g	5 oz
185 g	6 oz
220 g	7 oz
250 g	8 oz (½ lb)
280 g	9 oz
315 g	10 oz
345 g	11 oz
375 g	12 oz (¾ lb)
410 g	13 oz
440 g	14 oz
470 g	15 oz
500 g	16 oz (1 lb)
750 g	24 oz (1½ lb)
1 kg	32 oz (2 lb)

LIQUID MEASURES

METRIC	IMPERIAL
30 ml	1 fl oz
60 ml	2 fl oz
100 ml	3 fl oz
125 ml	4 fl oz
150 ml	5 fl oz (¼ pint/1 gill)
190 ml	6 fl oz
250 ml	8 fl oz
300 ml	10 fl oz (½ pint)
500 ml	16 fl oz
600 ml	20 fl oz (1 pint)
1000 ml	1¾ pints

CUP & SPOON MEASURES

METRIC	CUP / SPOON
1 ml	¼ tsp
2 ml	½ tsp
5 ml	1 tsp
15 ml	1 tbsp
60 ml	¼ cup
125 ml	½ cup
250 ml	1 cup

HELPFUL MEASURES

METRIC	IMPERIAL
3 mm	⅛ in
6 mm	¼ in
1 cm	½ in
2 cm	¾ in
2.5 cm	1 in
5 cm	2 in
6 cm	2½ in
8 cm	3 in
10 cm	4 in
13 cm	5 in
15 cm	6 in
18 cm	7 in
20 cm	8 in
23 cm	9 in
25 cm	10 in
28 cm	11 in
30 cm	12 in (1 ft)

HOW TO MEASURE

When using the graduated metric measuring cups, it is important to shake the dry ingredients loosely into the required cup. Do not tap the cup on the table, or pack the ingredients into the cup unless otherwise directed. Level top of cup with a knife. When using graduated metric measuring spoons, level top of spoon with a knife. When measuring liquids in the jug, place jug on a flat surface, check for accuracy at eye level.

OVEN TEMPERATURES

These oven temperatures are only a guide; lower degree of heat are given. Always check the manufacturers manual.

	°C (CELSIUS)	°F (FAHRENHEIT)	GAS MARK
Very Slow	120	250	1
Slow	150	300	2
Moderately Slow	160	325	3
Moderate	180	350	4
Moderately Hot	190	375	5
Hot	200	400	6
Very Hot	230	450	7

INDEX

Achari Murgh 66

Almond 82, 97-99, 245
- Ground 69
- Slivered 249, 257, 262

Aloo Gobi 7, 135

Aloo Jeera 136

Aloo Pattice 32

Appetizer 29-49, 227

Baingan Bharta 139

Baking powder 39, 40, 47

Balti Chicken Pasanda 69

Beetroot 108-109, 131

Bell Pepper
- Green 76, 85, 89, 136, 145, 154, 169
- Red 76, 117
- Yellow 76, 117

Black Tea Powder 265

Black Eyed Peas 157

Boiled Basmati Rice 163

Bombay 3-11, 16-17, 31, 86, 105-107, 233
- Andhra Pradesh 7
- British 4-5, 8-9, 71, 78, 105
- Calcutta 8
- Charles II 3-4
- Dutch Empire 4-5
- The East India Company 4, 9
- England 3, 78
- Good Bay 4
- Hindu 3-5, 131
- Indo-Chinese 5, 8, 11
  - Yang Tai Chow 8
- Karnataka 7
- Kerala 7, 122
- Koli 3-4
  - Fisher folk 3, 106-107
- Konkan 6
- Kung Pao 8
- Maharashtra 4, 223
  - Marathi 3-4

Bombay continued
- Mughal 3, 69, 94
  - Mughlai 15, 72, 94, 97
- Mumbai 4
- Muslim 5
- North Indian 6-7, 69, 132
- Parsi (parsee) 5, 8-9, 11-12, 105, 170, 191, 195, 210, 212, 214, 216, 219-220, 223, 257, 262
  - Freddy Mercury 9
  - Jamsetji Tata 9
  - Persis Khambatta 9
  - Ratan Tata 9
  - Zoroastrian 9
  - Zubin Mehta 9
- Port 4
- Portugal 3
  - Portuguese 3-5, 7-8, 71, 80
- Punjabi 6-7, 15, 157, 196
- Sassoon Dock 105, 107
  - Albert Abdullah David Sassoon 106
  - David Sassoon & Co., Ltd. 105
  - Fort Bombay 106
- Sikh 5
- South Indian 7, 173
- Street hawker 6
- Tamil Nadu 7
- Treaty of Bassein 3
- Treaty of Whitehall 3
- West 4-10, 15, 18, 31, 131, 223

Bread (Rotee)
- Bhatura/Pooris 141, 177, 179
- Chappati 110, 154, 177, 179, 187
- Naan 14, 15, 65, 79, 135, 177, 180
  - Garlic 7, 180
  - Plain, butter 7, 180
- Pappadum 43, 157, 177
- Paratha 58, 67, 69, 79, 136, 150, 177
  - Plain 183
  - Stuffed 184
- Roti 6, 7, 93, 139, 149, 177

Bread crumbs 36, 44, 48, 108, 113, 125, 215, 216

Broccoli 82, 149

Butter 7, 9, 16-17, 22, 65, 76, 86, 127, 153, 196
- Salted 16, 65, 76, 86, 127, 153
- Unsalted 16, 44, 48, 54, 79, 169, 180, 184, 187, 195, 250, 257

Butter Lettuce 108

Cabbage Salad 234

Cage free eggs 82, 85, 108, 113, 125, 196, 199, 207, 215-216, 219, 257

Carrots 48, 82, 146, 149, 184, 245, 249

Cashew nut 97, 146, 149, 203, 213

Cashew nut paste 72, 79, 98-99, 146, 153, 200

Cauliflower 135, 149

Celery 169, 215

Channa Masala 7, 140

Cheese 40, 44, 48, 108, 132, 219, 254
- Cheddar 110
- Grated 108

Cheese Fish Fillets with Hot Tomato Sauce 108

Chicken Biryani 164

Chicken Curry 7-8, 70

Chicken Korma 72

Chicken Liver Gravy with Gizzards 192

Chicken Lollipops 35

Chicken Tikka Kebab 76

Chicken Tikka Masala 7, 78-79

Chicken Vindaloo 80

Chickpea 40, 43, 61, 131, 140

Chutney 7, 18, 43, 44, 220, 227
- Mango 31, 61, 125
- Mint 31, 39-40, 47-48, 54, 58, 61, 76, 125, 220, 223
- Peach 125, 238
- Tamarind 18, 31, 36, 39-40, 47, 58, 61, 97, 113, 233
- Spicy Red 31, 40, 113, 230

Cilantro 32, 39, 44, 47-48, 57, 61-62, 66, 69-70, 72, 75, 79, 80, 82-83, 85, 89, 93, 97, 98, 99, 101, 110, 113, 117-118, 123, 125, 127, 131, 136, 139-141, 145-147, 154, 164-165, 169-171, 180, 184, 191, 193, 195, 199-200, 203-204, 210-211, 213, 215-216, 219-220, 227, 229, 237, 241

Coconut 67, 72, 122, 131, 227, 229, 245
- Milk 17, 83, 114, 122, 196
- Powder 70, 72, 121, 149, 196, 200, 203, 210, 220

Cookbook 8, 12, 15, 107

Cooking time 115, 127
- Gas range 15

Coomi 8-9
- Colaba Causeway 4, 8
- Farhang Irani 11
- Ideal Corner Restaurant 11, 106
- Leopold Café 8
- Taj Hotel 11

Cucumber 108-109, 131, 191, 237, 241

Cuisine 3, 5-8, 11, 16, 64, 72

Dal
- Pink Masur/Masoor Dal 195
- White Urad Dal/White Lentil 173
- Whole Black Lentil 117, 157
- Yellow Split Lentil 143

Dal and Spinach 143

Dessert 18, 245-246, 253-254

Dhansakh Dal 194

Dried Wheat Milk Powder 246

Dried Apricot 212-213

Drink 6, 10, 246, 266

Dry Jeera Chicken 75

Dum Jhinga Anari 110

East Indian Chicken Curry 82

Egg Bhurji 199

Egg Curry 196

Eggplant (aubergine/baingan) 36, 131, 139, 195, 210, 211

Eggplant Cutlets 36

Equipment
- Bamboo skewers 56, 61, 76, 86, 97
- Cheese Cloth 132
- Dutch Oven 164-165, 215-216
- Kulfi Ice Cream Mold 6, 258
- Popsicle Stick
- Pots, pans, skillets, griddle, wok 4, 6, 15, 22, 26, 43, 62, 89, 94, 117, 154, 169, 173, 177, 180, 183-184, 187, 204, 213, 223
- Rice Cooker 10, 169, 253
- Thread 76, 86, 97, 220-221

Eruch 8

Falooda 244

Falooda Sev 6, 246

Fish Cakes 113

Fish in Coconut Milk 114

Flour 17, 40, 48, 180, 245, 250
- Cake 35, 44, 179
- Corn 108-109
- Garbanzo Bean/Besan 39, 40, 61, 146
- Gram 39, 40, 43, 61, 146
- Maida 35, 44, 47, 179
- Plain 47, 179
- Wheat 177, 179, 183-184, 187
- White 85

Fish Tamatar 200

French Green Beans 82, 131, 149

Fried Brown Rice 208

Gajar Halwa 249

Garbanzo Bean 61, 140-141, 146

Garlic 7, 25, 82, 85, 121, 131, 140, 167, 169, 180

Garlic-Ginger Paste 8, 35, 54, 57-58, 61-62, 66, 69, 72, 75, 79-80, 85, 89, 93-94, 97-98, 110, 114, 117, 118, 121-122, 125, 135, 139, 140, 145-147, 149-150, 154, 157, 170, 195, 199, 200, 203-204, 210, 213, 215, 216, 220, 227

Garlic Chicken Dry 85

Ghee 16-17, 122-123, 153, 164-165, 180, 183, 187, 195, 249-250, 262

Ginger 25-26, 40, 72, 75, 82, 89, 93, 113, 117, 121, 131, 145, 153, 227, 238

Green Chicken Curry 203

Green Peas & Mushroom Rice 167

Grilled King Prawns with Stir-Fried Spices 117

Gulab Jamun 250

Heavy cream 17, 69, 79, 90, 97-98, 118, 146-147, 150, 153, 200, 258, 261

Herb, Shrimp & Fish Pulao Rice 168

Honey 11, 86, 94, 250, 258, 261

Honey Dates 18, 233

Honey Lemon Chicken 86

India
- History 3-4, 12, 107
- Indian 4-6

Ingredient 5, 8-10, 12, 16-18, 22, 57, 61, 145-147, 153, 184, 199, 227, 229
- Grocery, supermarket 16-17, 26, 32, 35, 39-40, 44, 47-48, 58, 61, 70, 76, 79, 82, 86, 101, 110, 113, 122, 145-146, 150, 153-154, 195, 210, 213, 220, 246, 250, 262

Jaggery 193, 210-211

Jhinga (small shrimp) Malai Curry 118

Kachumbar Salad 277

Kadhai Paneer 145

Karahi (Wok) Chicken 89

Kashmiri Lamb Rogan Josh 65

Kera-Per-Eda (Eggs and Fried Bananas) 207

Ketchup 44, 108-110, 153

Kheema Curry 204

Kheer 253

Khoya 254

Kofta Curry 146

Kolmi-No-Patio 210

Lagan-Nu-Custard 257

Lamb Chop 54

Lamb Curry 7, 57, 65

Lamb Jardaloo Salli Boti 212

Lamb Kathi Roll 58

Lamb Pulao 170

Lamb Seekh Kebab 61

Lamb Shank 62

Lemon 11, 35, 48, 61, 66, 76, 86, 94, 97, 108, 109, 110, 118, 125, 127, 132, 136, 140-141, 173, 191, 200, 220, 223, 229, 234, 250, 258, 261

Lime 6, 54, 58, 108, 114, 121, 127, 164-165, 170-171, 196, 203-204, 219, 227, 237, 261

Madras Fish Curry 121

Malabar Shrimp Curry 122

Mango 11, 90, 131, 258, 261, 266
- Chunks
- Cubed 261
- Powder 32, 40
- Pulp 90, 258,, 261, 266
- Puree 258

Mango Chicken Masala 90

Mango Ice Cream 258

Mango Lassi 266

Mango Mousse 261

Marathi 3-4

Marghi-Na-Farcha 214

Masala 7, 32, 54, 66, 79, 90, 140, 154, 179, 195-196
- Chaat 40, 48
- Dhansakh 194-195
- Garam 22, 35-36, 40, 48, 54, 61-62, 65, 69, 75, 79, 83, 85, 89, 118, 127, 135, 140, 145, 147, 150, 153-154, 170, 184, 193, 200, 204, 213, 216
- Tandoori 35, 76, 79, 86, 101

Masala Chai 265

Meat 6-8, 10, 15, 17-18, 20, 35, 47, 51-101, 108, 114, 131, 170, 204, 208, 212-213, 220, 223
- Chicken 5, 7-8, 10-11, 15, 26, 35, 66-101, 192-193, 203, 214-215, 164-165
  - Breast 66, 69, 75-76, 85-86, 94, 97, 101, 164
  - Chicken wings 35
  - Drumsticks 72, 94
  - Murgh 66, 76, 93-94
  - Liver 192-193
  - Thigh 89
  - Gizzard 192-193
- Fish (machhalee) 6, 8, 15, 105-106, 108, 113-114, 121, 168-169
  - Jumbo Prawn 69, 110, 117, 125, 210
  - Mahi-Mahi 127

Meat continued
- Fish (machhalee)
  - Salmon 127
  - Shrimp (jheenga) 106, 110, 117-118, 122-125, 168, 169, 210-211
  - Sole 200
  - White Pomfret 107, 220, 223
  - White Meat 72, 85, 108, 114, 220, 223
- Lamb 6, 7, 35, 54, 57, 58, 65, 195, 212
  - Cubed 170, 213
  - Memana 51-65
  - Minced 61, 204, 216
  - Shank 11, 62

Methi Murgh 93

Mint 108, 113, 131, 216, 219-220, 227, 229, 261

Mint Chutney 229

Murgh Mussalam 94

Mutton Kebab 216

Mushroom 6, 149, 167
- Button 167

Navrattan Korma 7, 149

Non-vegetarian 11, 132

Oil 8, 22, 43, 105, 139, 184
- Cooking 16-17, 47, 57, 62, 65-66, 69-70, 72, 75, 80, 85, 89-90, 93-94, 98, 113-114, 117-118, 121-122, 125, 135-136, 140, 143, 145-146, 150, 153-154, 157, 167, 170, 173, 193, 196, 199-200, 203, 204, 207-208, 210, 213, 215, 219, 220, 223
- Extra virgin oil 16, 54, 58, 61, 65, 97, 101, 123, 234
- Frying 32, 35-36, 39-40, 44, 47-48, 85, 108, 125, 179, 216, 251

Onion Bhajias (Pakodas) 39

Orange juice 58

Organic whole milk 17, 44, 250, 254

Palak (Saag) Paneer 7, 150

Paneer 6-8, 26, 40, 44, 48, 132, 144-146, 150, 152-154

Paneer Makhani 153

Paneer Pakoda 40

Paneer Tawa Masala (Paneer Bhurji) 154

Parsi Poro 219

Parsi Sev 262

Parsley 108-109, 169

Patra-Ni-Machi 220

Peach 125, 238

Peach Chutney 238

Pistachio Nuts 245-246, 250, 251, 253, 257

Plaintain (banana) 131, 207, 220-221

Pomegranate Seed 110

Potato 6, 8, 32, 43-44, 47, 80, 113, 124-125, 135-136, 143, 146, 149
- Potato Shoestrings (Sali) 212-213

Punjabi Dal (Black Dal) 157

Raisin 44, 207, 213, 242, 249, 253, 262
- Dark 44
- Golden 44, 213, 253

Raisin Aloo Paneer Rolls 44

Recipe 6, 8, 12, 15-16, 25, 40, 44, 47-48, 58, 65, 76, 79, 86, 101, 107, 113, 117, 122-123, 125, 131, 145, 150, 153-154, 164, 167, 169, 171, 173, 196, 208, 223, 245, 253

Red-Gold Saffron Chicken 98

Red Pumpkin 195

Reshmi Kebab (Silken Kebab) 97

Relish 225, 227

Rice (Chaaval) 7, 10, 15, 43, 65, 71, 157, 159-173, 203, 208, 210-211, 253
- Basmati Rice 70, 72, 83, 89, 114, 117-118, 143-145, 153, 164, 195, 203, 208, 211, 253

Rose
- Petal 246
- Syrup 246
- Water 207, 250, 253

Saffron 6, 18-19, 65, 98, 164, 170-171, 250, 253, 258

Salad 11, 16, 131
- Cabbage 234
- Kachumbar 191, 237

Salt
- Kosher 36
- Sea 36

Samosa 6, 47
- Meat 204
- Vegetarian 47

Shrimp Kebab 125

South Indian Lemon Rice 173

Spice 3, 6, 8, 10, 16-18, 21, 26, 32, 36, 40, 43, 47-48, 66, 70-71, 80, 85, 110, 117-118, 124-125, 127, 131, 135-136, 139-140, 143, 149-150, 157, 170, 193, 199, 207, 210, 223, 238, 265
- Anise Seed
  - Saunf 66
- Bay Leaf 21, 65, 79, 98, 149, 164-165, 169, 208

Spice continued
- Black Peppercorn 21, 26, 75, 125, 220
  - Ground 75, 125, 220
- Cardamom 22, 26, 57, 65, 69-70, 75, 93-94, 98, 118, 149, 153, 167, 170-171, 203, 238, 249-250, 253, 257, 265
  - Black 22, 26
  - Green 22, 57, 90, 94, 98, 153, 170, 171, 203
- Chili 7-8, 157
  - Dried 21, 122, 145, 173, 238
  - Green 32, 39, 69-70, 75, 89, 93, 97, 113-114, 118, 122, 125, 136, 143, 146, 150, 154, 195, 199, 203, 210, 215-216, 219-220, 229-230, 237, 241
  - Red 21, 47-48, 57, 66, 72, 80, 82, 94, 110, 122, 136, 139, 145, 164, 173, 184, 193, 238
  - Powder 21, 26, 35-36, 39-40, 44, 47-48, 54, 58, 61, 65-66, 69-70, 72, 80, 85, 93, 98, 110, 117-118, 121-122, 135-136, 139, 143, 145, 150, 153-154, 164, 170, 184, 193, 195-196, 200, 213, 215-216, 219, 223, 230, 233
- Cinnamon 21-22, 26, 65, 69-70, 82, 86, 90, 93, 117, 140, 167, 215, 249, 265
  - Stick 21, 69-70, 82, 90, 93, 117, 140, 167, 208, 265
  - Powder 61, 70, 80, 86, 215, 249
- Clove 21-22, 25-26, 57, 65, 70, 82, 93-94, 121, 140, 164, 167, 169-171, 215, 249, 265
  - Powder 94, 164, 215, 249
- Coriander
  - Seeds 26, 62, 75, 82, 89, 139, 145
  - Powder 21, 40, 54, 66, 70, 90, 121-122, 127, 135, 140, 145-146, 150, 154, 164, 196, 203, 223, 238

Spice ...continued
- Dal Makhani Powder....157
- Cumin....32, 39-40, 47, 58, 62, 65, 69-70, 75, 80, 82, 90, 110, 118, 121-122, 135-136, 139-140, 143, 146, 150, 154, 167, 171, 196, 203, 210, 220, 229, 233
- Curry....7, 8, 17, 47, 57, 65, 70-72, 79-80, 82, 90, 98, 114, 118, 121-123, 131, 136, 139-140, 144, 146, 152, 173, 195-196, 203-204, 210
  - Leaf....70, 80, 114, 118, 121-123, 131, 136, 139, 173, 195, 210
  - Powder....80
- Fennel....65, 117, 196
- Fenugreek (kasoon methi)....21, 26, 66, 89, 93, 121, 131, 145, 150, 153, 195, 166
  - Fresh....93, 195
  - Dried....26, 89, 145, 150, 153
- Fresh Thyme....169
- Mustard Seed....21, 47, 118, 121-122, 135, 173, 210, 234
- Nutmeg....21, 61, 65
  - Nutmeg Powder....207, 249, 257
- Onion seed....39, 66, 238
- Paprika....26, 36, 79, 117, 121, 127, 230, 241
- Poppy seed....121, 125, 20
- Star Anise....21, 65, 169
- Turmeric....21, 36, 39, 44, 54, 66, 70, 72, 90, 114, 121-122, 127, 135-136, 139-140, 143, 146-147, 149, 170, 173, 184, 195-196, 203-204, 213, 215-216, 219, 223
- White Pepper powder....110, 219

Spicy Red Chutney....230

Spinach....143, 150, 179

Sugar....9, 18, 57, 65, 79, 86, 90, 98, 108-109, 118, 153, 169, 173, 179, 180, 193, 203, 207-208, 210, 213, 220, 229, 233, 238, 241, 245-246, 249-250, 253, 257-258, 261-262, 265-266

Sunflower Seed....200

Sweet Corn....8, 149

Sweet Green Pea....167

Sweet Lassi....266

Tabasco Sauce....108-109

Tandoori Chicken....101

Tandoori Cooking 7, 15, 26, 35, 76, 79, 86, 101, 127

Tandoor oven 6, 7, 15, 61, 76, 117, 127, 177, 180

Tandoori Fish....127

Tamarind Chutney....233

Tamarind....18, 131, 221
- Tamarind Pulp....121-122, 233

Tareli Machi....223

Tomato....8, 57, 80, 82-83, 139, 143, 149, 167, 170, 191, 193, 196, 199, 204, 230, 237
- Chopped....62, 89, 93, 121-122, 135, 140, 145, 147, 150, 153-154, 195, 200, 204, 210, 213, 230
- Grape....241
- Pureed....65, 70, 79, 108-109, 114, 118, 140, 146-147, 153, 157, 169, 200
- Sauce....48, 108-109

Traditions
- Traditional, traditions....5, 8, 11-12, 15, 17, 97, 117, 132, 170, 177, 180, 210, 216

Tukmaria Seed....246

United States
- California....11, 234
  - Bombay Coast....11, 86
  - San Diego....11, 131
  - University of California at San Diego....11, 78

Vanilla Extract....257-258, 262

Vanilla Ice Cream....248

Vinegar....213
- Apple Cider....121, 238
- Malt....54, 110
- White....36, 80, 193, 210, 220, 230

Vegetarian (Shaakaahaaree) 7, 11, 129, 131-132

Veggie Balls....48

Vermicelli....246, 262

Whole Wheat Semolina
- Suji....47-48, 179

Worchester Sauce....18, 108-109

Yogurt....16-17, 26, 54, 58, 62, 65-66, 72, 76, 86, 93, 98, 101, 110, 117, 127, 164, 170, 173
- Cream top....72, 266
- Greek....69, 266
- Raita....164, 183-184, 241

Yeast....179-180

Yogurt Rita....241

Zucchini....149